The Great Archimedes

Mario Geymonat

The Great Archimedes

R. Alden Smith
Translator and Editor

BAYLOR UNIVERSITY PRESS

Cover and book design based on the original Italian edition.
Cover image: "A Scholar" (oil on canvas), Fetti or Feti, Domenico
(1589–1624) / Gemaeldegalerie Alte Meister, Dresden, Germany
/ © Staatliche Kunstsammlungen Dresden / The Bridgeman Art
Library International

Originally published as *Il Grande Archimede* by Mario Geymonat
(ISBN 978-88-88249-23-0). Copyright 2008 by Sandro Teti
Editore.

Library of Congress Cataloging-in-Publication Data

Geymonat, Mario.
  [Grande Archimede. English]
  The great Archimedes / Mario Geymonat ; foreword by Zhores
Alferov ; preface by Luciano Canfora ; translated and edited by R.
Alden Smith.
      p. cm.
  Includes bibliographical references and index.
  ISBN 978-1-60258-311-5 (pbk. : alk. paper)
  1. Archimedes. 2. Scientists--Greece--Biography. I. Title.
  Q143.A62G4913 2010
  509.2--dc22
  [B]
                                          2010038746

Printed in the United States of America on acid-free paper with a
minimum of 30% pcw recycled content.

To my father and my son, both Ludovico

TABLE OF CONTENTS

FOREWORD

Archimedes is one of the most original and prolific scientists in the history of humankind. Because of a prodigious mathematical imagination and a thoroughly advanced methodology, Archimedes was able to demonstrate proofs for an amazing set of geometrical theorems: on the quadrature of the circle, on the measurement of cylinders and spheres, on spirals, on conoids and other spherical shapes, and even on semi-regular polyhedrons.

In arithmetic, Archimedes made great strides by determining, with extraordinary precision, very large numbers, such as the number of grains of sand necessary to fill the entire universe. Archimedes' contributions to physics and engineering are equally important, especially his research on the lever, on the laws of mechanics, and on optics. He possessed an unparalleled ability to invent and build complex machines for both civilian and military purposes, such as the winch, the screw pump, some catapults, and possibly even "burning mirrors."

Like Galileo in the seventeenth and Einstein in the twentieth century, Archimedes responded to the civil and political problems of his day with intelligence and passion. He thus courageously devoted himself to defending his hometown, Syracuse, one of the largest and most advanced cities of antiquity. Tragically, it was precisely when the city had fallen into the hands of the invading Romans (212 BC) that Archimedes met his end, brutally killed by a soldier who could not fathom how, in so perilous a situation, Archimedes persisted in occupying himself with abstract geometry.

Historians, orators, architects, and poets, whether Greek or Roman (e.g., Polybius, Plutarch, Cicero, Vitruvius, and Virgil), included Archimedes in their writings. His reputation expanded throughout the medieval period. Moreover, during the Renaissance and the Reformation, translations of Archimedes' texts coupled with thorough study of his theorems provided a strong foundation for the development of modern science.

A number of rare and beautiful illustrations enrich Mario Geymonat's pleasantly uncomplicated yet dexterous *The Great Archimedes*. This work represents a major contribution to the dissemination of knowledge about and admiration for this extraordinary historical figure. With this fresh contribution, Geymonat ensures that Archimedes will continue to be an example of mathematical genius for generations to come, and will continue to stimulate further interest in complex and difficult scientific questions. In this way, the great Archimedes, our learned colleague from antiquity, offers confidence to a new generation as it faces its own challenges.

—Zhores Alferov

PREFACE

In this book, Archimedes is considered with great erudition from every point of view, including his contribution to the development of weaponry. In this regard, though he was not necessarily disposed to offering practical applications of his work, Archimedes proves to have been valuable and useful to his fellow men, as his machines engendered fear even in the Romans when they attacked his hometown. Among his most fascinating contrivances—the reality of which has been both called into question or attributed to exaggeration—are the famous "burning mirrors."

Mario Geymonat demonstrates the ways in which even the amatory poet Catullus was influenced by Archimedes, who proved to be a frequent source of fascination for writers, beginning with Plutarch. That biographer speaks about him at some length in the *Life of Marcellus*. Archimedes was even the subject of a romanticized biography in the work of the scientific writer Egmont Colerus (1888–1939), a pseudonym of Egmont von Geldern. Colerus was, among other things, the author of the well-known *Von Pythagoras bis Hilbert* (*From Pythagoras to Hilbert*), *Die Epochen der Mathematik und ihre Baumeister* (*The Ages of Mathematics and Their Pioneers*), and the equally famous *Vom Punkt zur vierten Dimension: Geometrie für jedermann* (1939), translated from its subtitle into English by B. C. and H. F. Brookes as *Mathematics for Everyman* (in Italian, *Il romanzo della geometria*). Colerus also wrote a travel novel, published in 1926, entitled *Zwei Welten* (*Two Worlds*), and a widely circulated biography in 1934 entitled *Leibniz: Der Lebensroman eines weltumspannenden Geistes*.

Colerus entitled his book about Archimedes *Archimedes in Alexandria* (1939, reprinted in 1941 and 1950 by the Viennese publisher Zsolnay). The title reveals that Colerus' idea was to focus his biography of Archimedes on the scientist's dealings in Alexandria. At the height of the third century BC, that city was governed by a powerful Hellenistic monarchy and served as a cultural center of both literature and science. Here Archimedes had a fruitful interchange with the geographer Eratosthenes, the Greek mathematician Dositheus of Pelusium, and the Greek astronomer Conon of Samos. He speaks of Conon with the sincere affection of a student in a prefatory letter addressed to Dositheus:

> With regard to those theorems that you sent with Conon, the proofs of which you charged me to illustrate, the majority are in the books that Heraclides had brought to you, while the others are in the book that I am now sending you. Do not let it surprise you, however, that I only publish them now, for I had first wanted to show their genuineness to mathematicians. . . . But, before these experiments could be performed, our friend Conon died, and he certainly would have known how to illustrate them much better than I and, with his other discoveries, would have been in a position to advance the study of geometry.

Colerus' book, defined by Coppola as "a long fantasy novel," plunges Archimedes (and the reader) into the midst of the Greco-Egyptian capital of the Ptolemaic seat of power. Archimedes would have come to Alexandria after having been hired by Ptolemy II, and he must have lived there for quite a while until he was recalled home, when Syracuse was threatened by the Romans (213–212 BC).

Thus we see an Archimedes "in the upper room of the library and of the Museum," where he would have taken over the role Euclid had previously held. According to Colerus' imaginative reconstruction, "two women, Reality and Truth, revealed to Archimedes the secrets of science." Curiously, Professor Coppola concludes his review of Colerus' work with an enigmatic allusion: "Behold," he writes, "I think I have understood how it is that he [Archimedes] said one day that by leveraging a single point he could raise up the world (*da ubi consistam, caelum terramque movebo*), and why, without resentment [sic!] he was driven to burn enemy ships with a device that he kept saying would be 'a machine from hell.'" I have always wondered what he really intended with these words, whether these stark and unexpected final words did not contain some further message.

—

Could no link have existed, then, between the more or less permanent residence of Archimedes in Alexandria and his deep commitment to the defense of Syracuse against the Roman siege? It is likely that, when so few scraps of evidence are available, our data will be not entirely clear and are possibly even corrupt; nevertheless, it is useful to recall the situation of Syracuse between the first and second Punic War. After the naval victory of Lutatius Catulus at the Aegades Islands (241 BC), Sicily came to Rome as a province. Two Sicilian cities, however, Syracuse and Messina, which remained faithful to their treaties with Rome and thus had maintained their status as "allies," were exempted from taxation. Thus began the practice, so common then in Roman foreign policy, of holding as bound "allies" some powerful cities (such as Syracuse) that then maintained a semblance of independence within the framework of Roman sovereignty. When, after the Battle of Cannae (216 BC), Hannibal increasingly seemed to become the master of southern Italy (Lucania, Brutium, Tarentum), and while the Carthaginians also undertook the invasion of Sicily (Lilybaeum), Syracuse chose to defect (213 BC) from her powerful ally at a critical point. It seemed that a counterattack of the Greek world had begun. For Archimedes there could be no doubts.

—*Luciano Canfora*

TRANSLATOR'S PREFACE

As translator and editor, I would like'to thank first Mario Geymonat for the opportunity to encounter the great Archimedes in a meaningful way through his Italian original, *Il Grande Archimede*. I would also like to thank my conscientious assistants Stephen Margheim, Ben Smith, and Faith Wardlaw, for their fine suggestions and careful attention to detail for the editing and translating of the volume. Mrs. Alex Tomecek and Mrs. Thelma Mathews were also wonderfully helpful with numerous important details. Thanks, too, to Scott Wilde (Baylor) and, in Italy, to Anna Lombardo Geymonat, Piergiacomo Petrioli, and Gianni Profita, all of whom in various ways facilitated my work on this project. At Baylor University Press, Dr. Carey Newman, editor, and his staff have been very accommodating throughout the project, which they brought to publication in a timely fashion. I would also like to express my appreciation to Thomas Hibbs, dean of the Honors College, Dean Lee Nordt, Vice-Provost Truell Hyde, and Provost

Elizabeth Davis. I thank Mr. Lou Penge for being the first inspiration of this project. I wish to dedicate my translation to the person who introduced me not only to the classics but also to Italy, Professor Philip North Lockhart of Dickinson College. To him I owe more than I can say.

—*R. Alden Smith*

I

THE ADVENTUROUS LIFE OF A REMARKABLE SCIENTIST

Archimedes was the greatest mathematician of classical antiquity and among the greatest scientists of all time. Endowed with remarkable intuition and audacity, Archimedes subjected his discoveries to rigorous and logical self-scrutiny [plates 1 and 10b]. A man of his time, he was so devoted to his own people and civic life that countless anecdotes about him have been preserved. Such tales, some two thousand years later, are still charming and entertaining.

Let us consider one example. The second-century AD biographer Plutarch transmits this account:

> Therefore there is no reason to disbelieve the things which have been said concerning Archimedes. For example, charmed by a certain household Siren, he kept forgetting to eat and to care for his body. When the servants dragged him forcibly to the bathroom to wash and anoint him, he often drew a picture of some geometric figures in the ashes from the heater, and as soon

as they had smeared him with oil, he traced some lines on his own limbs with his finger. [*Life of Marcellus* 17; cf. plate 3]

Archimedes was born in 287 BC in Syracuse when the city was one of the largest and most powerful in the Mediterranean basin [fig. 1]. He was a relative and friend of Hiero II, his elder contemporary, who, by 271, had become the tyrant of Syracuse. Archimedes' father, Phidias, was an astronomer: he taught his son how to determine the ratio between the diameter of the sun and the moon. Certainly Phidias taught him the first elements of mathematics, which Archimedes later perfected in Alexandria, the intellectual capital of the world. He moved to this city in approximately 243 BC. Less than thirty years before, Theocritus, the greatest poet of Syracuse and founder of the bucolic genre, had relocated to the same cultural center.

Though Archimedes would ultimately not settle in Egypt, his time in Alexandria was vital for his formation, for there he joined a circle of scientists, all of whom belonged to the generation that followed immediately on that of the famous mathematician Euclid. Chief among those he befriended was the geographer Eratosthenes of Cyrene, to whom he would later dedicate his *Method*. Others of his colleagues were the astronomer Conon of Samos, whom he always held in high regard, and Dositeus, to whom he dedicated the treatise *On the Sphere and the Cylinder*, as well as *On Spirals* and *On Conoids and Spheroids*. With these colleagues Archimedes exchanged letters from Sicily, testing their work before offering them a definitive response. As a result, they were willing to discuss their ideas with him and suggest possible changes and improvements.

Archimedes showed ingenuity in his many important discoveries, some of which, since they can be dated earlier than him, are attributed to him only by legend. Nevertheless, many of these attributions are not without firm

FIGURE I

Statue of "The Great Archimedes" by Zurab Tsereteli.

historical grounding, such as the construction of some modern weaponry (cf. chap. 7), the discovery of the principle of the lever (chap. 3), and the law relating to bodies immersed in a liquid (chap. 4).

Archimedes wrote in Doric, the Greek dialect of Syracuse; at Alexandria, by contrast, the literary dialect would have been Attic. Archimedes' language and his literary dialect were thus passed down through the centuries. Though formulated in the impersonal language of mathematics, Archimedes' style has a surprisingly personal tone, described by Plutarch:

> For it is impossible, in geometry, to find harder and deeper hypotheses being treated in simpler and clearer terms. With regard to Archimedes, some attribute this to his inherited talent, while others think that he did it by working tirelessly, imagining that he achieved each of his individual accomplishments easily and adroitly. No one could, by effort alone, have discovered such mathematical proofs, and yet, as soon as anyone had learned from Archimedes, he had the impression that he himself could be successful in similar research. Thus, the road on which Archimedes led his followers toward demonstrated proof was smooth and easy. [*Life of Marcellus* 17]

It should be noted, of course, that the original texts of Archimedes describe the mathematical problems in a way significantly different from those of today because he did not have access to our modern algebraic symbolism (which was created in the seventeenth century). Instead, Archimedes employed, in general terms, a language of formulas, albeit a language less precise than we might wish (in fact the diagrams we find in his works are drawings that were, in all likelihood, modified by later copyists). Moreover, unlike those of Euclid, the works of Archimedes did not have a specific didactic purpose: he leaves out points of minutiae, instead offering his reader some ways of thinking that are in fact anything but easy.

Syracuse's most famous scientist was certainly not content merely to give the final touch to material already entirely or partly known; rather he devoted himself passionately to innovative discoveries and inventions. Thus the scientific historian Antonio Favaro characterizes Archimedes' mathematical treatises:

> Archimedes' works are not, like those of many other geometers of antiquity, merely collections or compilations. Archimedes is first and foremost a pioneer and inventor, and for the most part his surviving works contain new things created or discovered by him.[1]

Instead of gathering his research into book-length volumes, he wrote minor works on individual subjects. These he disseminated as tracts or letters addressed to famous scientists who were at that time living in Alexandria and whose friendship he enjoyed. What is more, there are quotes attributed to Archimedes that are found in numerous ancient scientific sources and refer more to the results than the specific form of presentation.

The works of Archimedes embrace various fields of science, foremost among them arithmetic, which is the principle form of his curious treatise entitled *The Sand Reckoner*. In this work he demonstrates how to calculate and to write large numbers, such as the grains of sand necessary to fill the entire celestial globe. His works also deal with different types of geometry, such as spirals. (Today, there is even a specific subsection of spirals known as "the spirals of Archimedes.") He also explained how to square both a circle and a parabola (chap. 2), and established for the first time the approximate value of Greek π; on the last of these numerous contributions, Reviel Netz comments:

Much of his work is devoted to the measurement of curved objects, and we can ask whether Archimedes would have been interested in a more general application of the problem of measurement of the circle with regard to other problems related to it, or instead would have hoped to be able to tackle in this way the problem of the circle; we cannot, however, answer this question again.[2]

In examining geometric figures, Attilio Frajese has noted that Archimedes "considered the flat shapes as those formed out of all the lines drawn on them in parallel fashion running in a certain direction, and similarly solid figures as formed (or 'filled') from their level sections parallel to a single secure location."[3]

More important for us is his handling of this subject in a treatise in two parts, entitled *On the Sphere and the Cylinder*, devoted to the comparison between the volume of a sphere and its circumscribed cylinder (chap. 5). Among his numerous booklets and many other fragments, some stand out as particularly important in the history of mathematics and physics. For example, *On Floating Bodies* provides a scientific basis for hydrostatics (cf. chap. 4). Though his works shaped the history of science, the history, or at least the exact chronology, of his works is difficult to establish, as they occur in different orders in the principal medieval testimonies.

As regards logical proof, Archimedes' expositions have great importance, for they are frequently based on the "exhaustive method" of pushing the argument to its logical conclusion (known as *argumentum ad absurdum*). For example, to prove that a certain area or volume has the value one has estimated rather than a greater or lesser value, a sequence of figures is inscribed or circumscribed on another to demonstrate that the result from either of these two assumptions would ultimately be absurd (see chap. 2).

The first significant application of this exhaustive method was that of Eudoxus of Cnidus in the fourth century BC. Already, by the early third century, this method was accepted as scientifically legitimate by Euclid, as can be seen in the twelfth book of the *Elements*. Archimedes, however, applied it more brilliantly than any of his predecessors, using it to demonstrate new and often unexpected results. This achievement earned him the enduring admiration of his contemporaries, who rightly considered his discoveries as, without doubt, the most logical outcome of that method.

It would be incorrect, however, to consider Archimedes an uncompromising champion of "strict logic" and thus an open opponent of those who—in the face of the slow and cumbersome method of exhaustion—proposed the use of faster intuitive processes. The historical reality is quite different: in his letter to Eratosthenes with which he opens his *Method on Mechanical Theorems* (discovered only at the beginning of the twentieth century, as will be enlarged on at the beginning of the eighth chapter), Archimedes explains with remarkable clarity how he has employed the method of exhaustion to establish a solid foundation for his own discoveries, while also using intuitive methods (a mixture of mathematics and physics) at the opening stage of his research.

This capacity to employ two different methods simultaneously shows both Archimedes' intellectual range and his fresh outlook upon scientific inquiry, which he regarded as if it were life itself, not simply research for research's sake. Precision was vital to Archimedes, whose bold mathematical feats have earned him the right to be regarded as a creative genius and one of the premier mathematicians of antiquity.

In the life and works of Archimedes, science and technology merge for the first time, with interdisciplinary advantages. The original contribution of the Syracusan scientist lay in his unique ability to unite the theoretical with the practical. He drew on his experience to undertake important experiments (such as the lever, specific weight, and others) that were performed carefully and later were systematically worked out in painstaking scientific treatises. Quite apart from mere theoretical considerations, these works reveal that in his research Archimedes availed himself of practical applications to solve specific problems.

In light of Archimedes' own affirmations in his *Method*, which could itself be a solid basis for the development of technologically and scientifically advanced civilization, one may wonder why he has not received the acclaim that he deserves. This is a complex question, which might generally be formulated thus: why, in the ancient world, did an advanced and mechanized civilization not develop since undoubtedly there were, if only to a limited extent, the theoretical conditions to do so?

For the particular case of Archimedes, one must not lose sight of his remarkable persistence, which transcended mere technical genius, a philosophical attitude that unfortunately did not sit well in Syracuse. Plutarch suggests as much when, after speaking of the engineering wonders of Archimedes, he praises the nobility of his talent, because of which he had consistently recused himself from writing popular treatises on practical issues:

> Therefore, believing the treatment of machines, like any other art that addresses immediate utility, to be ignoble and merely mechanical, Archimedes turned his attention exclusively to more ambitious studies, the beauty and abstraction of which are untainted by ordinary material needs. These studies, on the one hand, are not to be compared to one another, for each has an internal struggle between subject matter and proof, since the subject matter provides size and beauty, while

proof offers accuracy and extraordinary power. For it is impossible, in geometry, to find harder and deeper hypotheses being treated in simpler and clearer terms. [*Life of Marcellus* 17]

The reason that a mechanized civilization failed to develop in antiquity is a question that requires fuller inquiry involving consideration of the social stratification of the ancient world. Broadly speaking, Greco-Roman society was not subject to a strong compulsion to invent new machines. The reason for this is that that world had at its disposal the "natural machine" of slavery. That institution, which was sufficiently cost-effective to shirk mechanized assistance (at least at first), ultimately proved to be less convenient and efficient. Archimedes might well have considered himself lucky to be living in an age of rapid development of knowledge, and he likely understood that for years humankind had confronted one problem at a time, very often failing to achieve satisfying results.

With his *Method*, however, one proposition follows another in such a way that a layman can differentiate between them. Moreover, Archimedes demonstrates how each subsequent proposition deviates from the first. We know that many devices could be built based on new technological breakthroughs, but not everything had broad appeal. For example, the Roman army besieging Syracuse seemed to have paid little heed to the technology that they encountered in the siege. In fact, the ancients were loath to construct special automatic machines, for some slaves would no longer have known what to do.

Archimedes put his own technical ingenuity to the service of the city in peacetime as well as in war. Although he never founded a school, he cultivated knowledge more with the spirit of an engineer than with that of a professor. His active collaboration in the defense of Syracuse is well known. Claudius Marcellus, the Roman general, besieged

2A   2B

FIGURE 2

Obverse (2A) and reverse (2B) of a Roman denarius that represents
Marcus Claudius Marcellus, the general who conquered Syracuse
in 212 BC and was killed in an ambush by Hannibal in 208.
On the obverse, a portrait of Marcellus appears; he is portrayed as
an elderly man with a beard, indented cheeks, and a receding hairline.
Behind his head is depicted the "Trinacria," the three-legged symbol
of Sicily, the island he subdued. On the reverse is the commemoration
of the victory of Marcellus over the Insubri tribe of Gauls in 222 BC.
Marcellus is depicted as a fifth-time consul who carries to the temple
of Jupiter the spolia opima, *battle spoils that he had taken*
from the Gallic king, Viridomarus, whom he himself killed
in hand-to-hand combat.

---

the city between 213 and 212 BC [fig. 2A and 2B].[4] At the
battle's conclusion, Archimedes died at the hands of an
enemy soldier in the midst of a raging inferno. In this harsh
conflict, the first in which the Romans came face-to-face
with Greek scientific technology, Archimedes wanted to
leave a mark that would highlight the dichotomy between
the two worlds:

> Although so many base examples of wrath and avarice
> could be cited, it has been passed down to our mem-
> ory that, in the midst of a prodigious uproar caused by

soldiers running in different directions on the captured city's streets, Archimedes, still gazing upon the figures that he had traced in the sand, died at the hands of a soldier who was ignorant of who he was. [Livy, *Ab urbe condita* 35.31]

To the invader, the scientist would have cried, "don't disturb my circles." This is a proverbial expression found in reference to the intellectual with his head in the clouds who wishes to continue his work without distraction even when his situation has become unsustainable. According to a version in Plutarch:

> Some say that the Roman stood there with his sword intending to kill Archimedes immediately. Although the scientist looked at him with a suppliant's demeanor and asked him to delay for a short time that he might not have to leave behind an incomplete and insufficiently demonstrated experiment, the soldier dispatched him with no regard for his request. [*Life of Marcellus* 19; cf. fig. 3]

The account of Valerius Maximus is also interesting in this respect, offering a few more salient details:

> I would say that the activity of Archimedes would have even been more fruitful, except that same thing that had given him life had taken it from him: in fact Marcellus, after he had conquered Syracuse, while realizing that his victory was far from great, inasmuch as it was hindered by Archimedes' defensive weapons, was nevertheless fascinated with the extraordinary genius of Archimedes. Marcellus made a public declaration that whoever saved the scientist's life would garner as much glory for saving him as Marcellus himself had for being the conqueror of Syracuse. Meanwhile Archimedes, with his mind preoccupied and his eyes fixed upon the ground, was drawing some figures there, when a soldier who had broken into

FIGURE 3

No representation known with certainty to depict Archimedes survives from antiquity. The Naples National Archaeological Museum has a bust that was once believed to portray him but now has been discovered to represent the Spartan king Archidamus III. There is much doubt surrounding the authenticity of a mosaic representing a scientist intent on tracing lines in a container placed on a table, while a Roman soldier is about to stab him to death. It seems to have belonged to Jerome Bonaparte, the brother of Napoleon, who believed it to have been taken from the excavations of Herculaneum. It is, however, probably a nineteenth-century forgery crafted in Campania.

his home to raid it put his sword to his head and asked him who he was. Archimedes, however, desirous of solving the problem that he was studying, could not say his own name but, protecting the design traced in the dust with his hands, said, "Please, do not disturb this." Thus, having given the impression of disregarding the superiority of his conqueror, Archimedes was beheaded, so that he mingled the features of his formula with his blood. And so the same passion that made a gift of his life took it in the end. [*Memorable Deeds and Sayings* 8.7.7]

Certainly the murder of Archimedes was a page in a less than glorious chapter of Roman history. The Roman general Marcellus, who can be officially excused from the crime, undertook the construction of a tomb to Archimedes with a representation of a cylinder with a sphere, effecting an allusion to the most famous mathematical work of the Syracusan scientist.

Moreover, the victorious Roman general did not fail to transfer to Rome the large and complex planetarium built by the scientist. "No . . . never again was such huge war booty brought home," as Cicero testifies with a touch of shame a century and a half later (*De re publica* 1.21).[5]

THE MYSTERIOUS GREEK LETTER π

It is well known that the Greek letter π (pi) is the symbol indicating the ratio between the circumference and the diameter or radius of a circle.[1] Its numerical value therefore solves the problem of the *rectification of the circumference* and the corresponding measurement of the *squaring of a circle*. This link between a *straight line* and a *curved line*, in a corresponding manner between a *polygon* and a *circle*, is already stated in the first of only three theorems demonstrated in Archimedes' *Measurement of a Circle*:

> The area of any circle is equal to a right triangle that has a right-angle side equal to the radius and the other right-angle side equal to the circumference of the circle. [see fig. 4]

The measurement of the lines corresponding to the curve of the circle in respect to its diameter or radius profoundly intrigued both ancient and modern mathematicians, and the ancients tried in various ways to move this complex matter

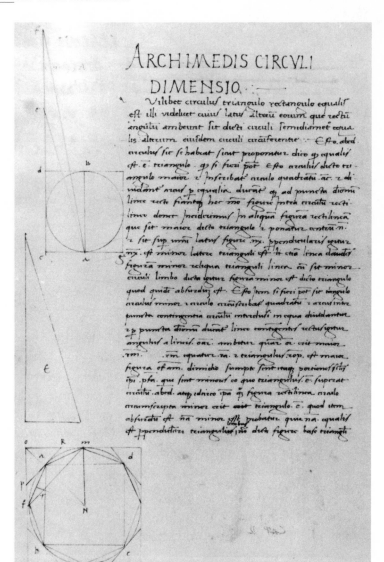

FIGURE 4

The beginning of Measurement of a Circle *in a copy of the Latin
translation of Jacopo of Cremona. The translation was rendered in
approximately 1450 on the order of Pope Nicholas V and was used by,
among others, Piero della Francesca and Leonardo da Vinci
(Venice, Biblioteca Marciana, no. 327, f. 106v).*

toward a satisfying, if somewhat mysterious, agreement. The Bible suggests that the relationship between the radius and half of a circle's circumference would be equal to *three*,[2] and one finds that many in antiquity were willing to settle for a generic, inaccurate measurement. Among these was the Latin poet Marcus Manilius (fl. at the beginning of the first century AD), who dedicates three verses of his *Astronomica* to the topic:

> Wherever a circle is cut through the center, a third of its circumference is then created by dividing the full sum of the circumference by the slight difference. [1.545–47]

Some ancient mathematicians tried to achieve the desired results by easily identifying curved lines with those broken into a large number of sides, and curved surfaces with a superficial polyhedron having many faces. But the transition from the broken line to the curved line or from the polyhedral surface to the true curve implies the leap from the finite to the infinite (only when the number of sides of the broken line becomes infinite can it be argued that it comes to be identified with the arc on which it is inscribed).

As Geoffrey E. R. Lloyd has explained, Archimedes' general approach is twofold:

> He uses both inscribed and circumscribed figures with a view to compressing them to a point where they coalesce with the curved figure to be measured.[3]

Specifically, Archimedes assumes, in his less-than-perfect calculation of π, the perimeter of a regular polygon inscribed within the circumference, and as the excess value, that of a regular polygon circumscribed around it. He separated the number of sides from the hexagons and then, one after another, doubled that number, considering the inscribed and circumscribed polygons on the circle respectively at 12, 24, 48, and 96 sides, recognizing that in this way he would still be able to fix the progression. For Archimedes, the higher and lower limits between which π must be measured are respectively 3 $\frac{1}{7}$ and 3 $\frac{10}{71}$:

> The circumference of each circle is triple the diameter and less than one-seventh of the diameter, and yet greater than ten seventy-firsts. [*Measurement of a Circle*, proposition 3]

Therefore, using decimal numbers, he is proposing a measurement just between 3.14084507 and 3.142857142, a figure remarkably close to the value we give π today.

Archimedes was the first Greek scientist to make use of fractions in the field of mathematics, since prior to Archimedes the Platonic concept of the indivisible unit held sway. Simply put, before Archimedes, fractions were not considered from a scientific point of view and fell only to merchants and their commerce.

Archimedes' short but dense work entitled *Size of the Circle* is without doubt one of antiquity's most exciting scientific texts. Not without reason, the mathematician Gaetano Fichera has defined it as "the most representative of his works."[4] In reality, the circumference and the diameter of the circle have proportions equally difficult to measure, and their relationship cannot be expressed simply as a ratio of integers (or rational numbers). The proof that π is an irrational number is owed to Johann H. Lambert, who came to that conclusion in 1768. More recently than Lambert, Ferdinand von Lindemann (1882) demonstrated that π is a transcendent number, a highly complex concept. Archimedes clearly had an intuition that it is virtually impossible for π to be a rational number and tried not to represent it by the ratio of two integers. Nevertheless, he sought to build a rational number that could be approximated as closely as possible, higher or lower than the number that π represents.

Fichera, cited above, goes on to say:

One can debate about whether Archimedes, as some argue, was the founder of modern infinitesimal analysis, but there is no doubt that he was the originator of modern numerical analysis, not designed—the way that so many use it—as experimental mathematics, but as a very rigorous mathematical system, representing the apex and supreme goal of all calculation.[5]

Certainly the emergence of the concept of infinity in Greek thought is connected to the calculation of the areas enclosed by curved lines (arcs of a circle, an ellipse, a parabola, etc.) and from that of the volumes enclosed by curved surfaces (surfaces of rotation obtained from those same lines),[6] as can be seen in figure 5.

The measurement of curved lines is addressed by Archimedes in his *Squaring of the Parabola*. The parabola is the best known of the conic sections, that is, of the curves described by the intersection of a cone or cones with different planes:

- if the plane is perpendicular to the axis of the cone, it is considered a circle;
- if the plane intersects both halves of a right circular cone at an angle parallel to the axis of the cone, it is considered a hyperbola;
- if the plane is not parallel to the axis, base, or generators of the cone, it is considered an ellipse;
- if the plane is parallel to one of the generators of the cone, it is considered a parabola.

In his *Squaring of the Parabola*, an ample and complex treatise, Archimedes comes to the fundamental conclusion that the area of the parabolic segment, namely of that portion of a parabola comprised by a line, and a section of a parabola is equal to four-thirds of an inscribed triangle

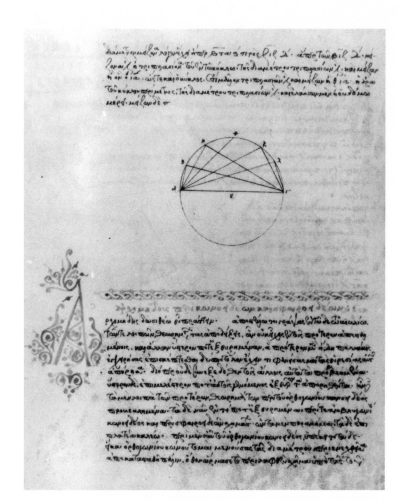

FIGURE 5

The end of Measurement of a Circle *and the beginning of* Conoids
and Spheroids *in a Greek manuscript of Archimedes written by
Cardinal Bessarion in the mid-fifteenth century
(Venice, Biblioteca Marciana, no. 305, f. 34v).*

that has the same base and height of the parabolic segment (Archimedes' twenty-fourth proposition). Archimedes dedicates this work to Dositheus, an Alexandrian mathematician who had once been a student of Conon, whose death he mentions with sadness in the letter of dedication. That letter concludes with the autobiographical testimony that he had first achieved this result by a mechanical device. Only afterwards did he prove it, strictly speaking, by geometry.

"GIVE ME A LEVER LONG ENOUGH AND I WILL MOVE THE WORLD"

Humankind has long known about the fundamental properties of the fulcrum point through the use of the balance and of levers of various types and sizes. In book I of his treatise *On the Equilibrium of Planes*, Archimedes treated the topic, in terms of mathematics and physics, with clarity:

> Commensurate sizes are in equilibrium if they are suspended at distances inversely proportional to their weights. [book I, proposition 6]

The Syracusan scientist offered a demonstration of this concept that was criticized by the late nineteenth-century scholar Ernst Mach, whose arguments are not entirely convincing.[1]

Archimedes is here referring to a balance (i.e., a rod suspended or supported at its midpoint in a horizontal position when it is in balance, on the ends of which weights are stationed). In response to the success he achieved by a complex system of levers, pulleys, and winches used to launch the great ship *Syracusia* (cf. chap. 7), Archimedes, amazed at the achievement, is said to have cried out enthusiastically:

Give me a lever long enough and I will move the world.[2]

Archimedes had realized that one could easily reduce the force required to move a given weight simply by increasing the distance in proportion to the point of application, that is, the fulcrum. It would thus be possible to lift a very heavy weight with limited exertion, even, theoretically, one as heavy as that of the earth, were it possible to find a fixed fulcrum point external to the earth [plate 3]. With regard to the basic propositions of static objects (i.e., the mechanics of the balance of solid bodies) this demonstration is rigorously deductive and scientifically innovative: to explain this Archimedes had to expound on the concepts of *balance* and *center of gravity* in geometric terms and in terms of a theory of proportions. We are therefore confronted with an assertion of a quantitative measurement that is itself subject to physics, namely the "law of the lever," according to which two variables are in equilibrium when the ratio of their distances from the fulcrum is the reciprocal of the ratio between their weights. For example, if the weights standing in relation to one another are at 2 to 3, their position on the lever ought to be in a ratio of 3 to 2 [fig. 6].

In the remainder of books I and II of *On the Equilibrium of Planes*, Archimedes treats the establishment of centers of gravity of various shapes of planes, such as the parallelogram ("the center of gravity of any parallelogram is the point where the diagonals intersect," book I, proposition 10), the triangle ("the center of gravity of any triangle is the point at which lines drawn from the vertices to the mid-points of the sides intersect," proposition 14), the trapezoid (proposition 15), and the parabolic segment or polygon inscribed on it (to their centers of gravity Archimedes dedicated the entirety of book II).

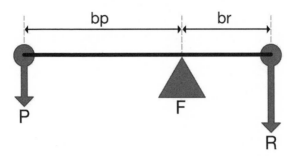

FIGURE 6

The lever is a simple device that consists of a stiff "pole" that turns upon a fixed point called a fulcrum (F). At each extremity of the pole one force is applied. One end bears "resistance" (R) and the other countervailing "power" (P). The distance from the fulcrum to the resistance is called the "resistance arm" (br), and that between the power and the fulcrum is called the "power arm" (bp).

Polyhedrons are prominent among the geometric shapes that Archimedes explicitly engages. Less than a century earlier, Euclid had described the five regular polyhedrons in the thirteenth book of his *Elements*. He thus described these regular three-dimensional shapes, with all their sides of equal length, as formed from a single regular polygon. They are:

- the tetrahedron, with 4 equal faces formed by equilateral triangles (book XIII, proposition 13);
- the hexahedron (or cube), with 6 equal square faces (book XIII, proposition 15);
- the octahedron, with 8 equal faces formed by equilateral triangles, four of which meet at each vertex (book XIII, proposition 14);

- the dodecahedron, with 12 faces made up of equal regular pentagons, and 20 vertices and 30 edges altogether (book XIII, proposition 17);
- the icosahedron, with 20 faces formed by regular equilateral triangles, and 12 vertices and 30 edges altogether (book XIII, proposition 16).

According to testimony furnished to us in the fourth century AD by the mathematician Pappus of Alexandria, Archimedes was particularly concerned with semi-regular polyhedrons that can be inscribed in a sphere and possess a number of uncommon symmetries. The sides of these polyhedrons are still formed from equilateral and equiangular polygons, but are not of a single type; that is to say, Archimedes' formulation allowed for triangles, squares, other triangles, and pentagons, along with various other shape combinations. He discovered thirteen of these polyhedrons, which are indeed very few and are still known today as "Archimedean." To give some examples:

- the first of these semi-regular polyhedrons is formed by 4 triangles and 4 hexagons;
- the second is made up of 8 triangles and 6 squares;
- the sixth, which in mathematical terms is called a "truncated cuboctahedron," consists of 12 squares, 8 hexagons, and 6 octagons [fig. 7];
- the eighth, which in mathematical terms is called a "truncated icosahedron," is made up of 12 pentagons and 20 hexagons (its form is that of a soccer ball, where the black faces are usually pentagonal and the white hexagonal) [fig. 8];
- the eleventh consists of 20 triangles, 30 squares, and 12 pentagons;
- the thirteenth is formed by 80 triangles and 12 pentagons.[3]

As research allowed him to establish the shape of the sphere more accurately, Archimedes took an interesting path through a seemingly chaotic field of study, to which he sought to give an intelligent and innovative order.

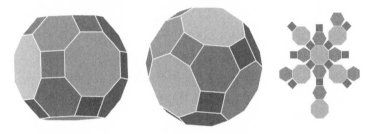

FIGURE 7

A truncated cuboctahedron, the sixth of the semi-regular polyhedrons distinguished by Archimedes, with 12 square faces:
8 hexagonal and 6 octagonal.
(This drawing and the other geometric designs are by Paolo Lazzarini.)

FIGURE 8

A truncated icosahedron, one of the semi-regular polyhedrons distinguished by Archimedes, with 12 pentagonal faces and 20 hexagonal. It is very similar to a sphere, and the shape of a soccer ball is modeled on it. The black areas on a soccer ball are normally pentagonal, while those that are white are normally hexagonal.

IV

EUREKA!

Were Archimedes to have used the word *Eureka!* each time he made a new discovery, he would have said it many times throughout his life. One of his most important discoveries involved the spiral, to which he directed an entire treatise entitled *On Spirals*.

The spiral is a flat curve, characterized by infinite twists that coninuously increase in a mathematical progression around a point. Such a curve cannot be constructed with a compass. Rather, one can conceptualize it with the movement of a vector that grows constantly out of a single space with every rotation on a given angle; or, it can be approximated by the winding of a tube that recalls the curl of a hair, the bark of a tree, or a vortex [plate 4]. Archimedes uses numerous such elegant and refined descriptions to address this topic in his treatise. In the letter of dedication to the Alexandrian mathematician Dositheus, Archimedes says that some theorems had been entrusted to him many years before by Conon, but "before they had had sufficient time to be developed by Conon, he had passed to another life." This specification allows us to place the work among the last writings of the scientist of Syracuse.

In the opening section of his treatise, Archimedes explained the mechanical generation of the spiral as a geometric line, still known to us today as the "spiral of Archimedes." Thus does Vitruvius, at the end of the first century BC, describe the Ionic capital in his treatise *De architectura* (*On Architecture*). As transmitted through Vitruvius, therefore, Archimedes would come to influence the architectural treatises of the Renaissance [fig. 9].[1]

A spiral proceeds from a point on a plane (called its origin or beginning) moving in uniform motion along a straight line, while rotating in a uniform circular motion around the point. To describe the spiral's motion, Archimedes gives the definitions of straight uniform motion, of circular uniform motion, and of their interaction. In proposition 1, this is calculated vis-à-vis the passage of time:

> If a point is moved with constant speed on a line, and two segments are assumed on this line, they will have between them the same ratio as the times in which the point moved across them [fig. 10].[2]

Turning to more characteristically geometric properties, Archimedes reaches some surprising results on *rings* and on *segments* that are limited by the turns of the spiral, particularly in his proposition 27:

> Of the area comprised of the spiral and the straight lines in rotation, the third revolution is twice the second, the fourth is triple, the fifth is a quadruple of the second, and always the area following is a multiple of the second area by successive integers, while the area covered by the spiral in the first revolution is the sixth part of that of the second revolution.

FIGURE 9

*The development of the spiral studied by Archimedes in an Ionic
capital of the Temple of Portunus (formerly known as Fortuna Virilis)
in Rome, constructed during the second century BC and preserved
mostly intact.*

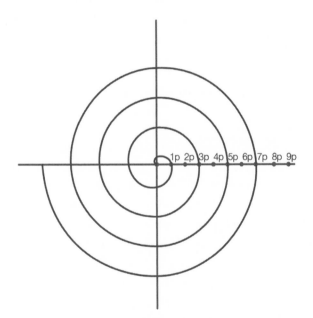

FIGURE 10

*A clockwise spiral, one of the curves studied by Archimedes
with great innovation.*

Moreover, it seems that the scientist not only attached importance to the legitimacy of the objects with which he was concerned but reckoned that, however complicated they were, they could be measured. The more complex an object appeared to him, the more his intelligence was stimulated:

> *On Spirals* can perhaps be considered Archimedes' finest work with regard to his inventiveness, of which he gave a demonstration, and to the brilliantly simple results that he presented, and the very fine organization that he orchestrated.[3]

Many of Archimedes' discoveries in the field of statics and hydrostatics seem to have originated from a search for technical efficiency. Particularly noteworthy is the account of Archimedes' being faced with a difficult problem to which he was able to discover an unforeseen solution (plate 5). This sudden discovery made him exclaim with enthusiasm "*Eureka, Eureka!*" which, in Greek means, "I have found it, I have found it!" It is an expression used cross-culturally to this day and often without the user's knowledge of its origin in antiquity (one thinks, for example, of its association with the California Gold Rush). For Archimedes, it was first associated with the discovery of the concept of specific weight, to which Archimedes did not give a precise name, and the testing that confirmed that weight.

Even if this rich story is apocryphal in part, it is worth recalling in detail. The Latin writer Vitruvius (1C BC) tells the story: Hiero II of Syracuse ordered that a gold crown be fashioned as a token of thanks to the gods, by whose beneficence he believed that he had become the ruler of Syracuse. Hiero himself was to provide the gold, and in short order he received the item. He learned, however, that the goldsmith had filched some of the gold, even though the crown had the same weight of material delivered by him. It was possible that some gold had been replaced with silver, a metal known to be less valuable, albeit not in such quantity as to change the color of the article and to give clear evidence of the deception. Hiero asked Archimedes

> to assume the task of reflecting about this on his behalf. It happened that, as he began to think about it, he went into the bathroom and there, when he lowered himself into the tub, he noticed that this action displaced a quantity of water equivalent to the volume of his body. This showed him the way to solve the problem: he did not linger, but rather jumped out of the tub with a shout of joy, and nude as he was, went rushing toward the house. He kept proclaiming loudly that he had discovered what he was seeking. As he ran, he kept crying out in Greek, "Eureka! Eureka!" ("I have found it, I have found it!").[4] [*De architectura* 9, *pref.* 10; cf. fig. 11]

The account of Vitruvius continues:

> From this early stage in his research, it is said that he then manufactured two ingots, each of the same weight as the crown, one of gold and the other of silver. After this, he filled a large vessel to the brim with water and dropped the silver ingot into it. This displaced a quantity of water equal to its volume when it sank into the vessel. He then removed the ingot and added back the missing quantity of water, measuring it with a sextarius [roughly a pint], so that the previous level was restored right up to the brim. In this way he discovered the weight of silver corresponding to a given quantity of water [i.e., the specific gravity]. After this experiment, similarly he lowered the gold ingot into the full container and, after removing it, he added the missing water by measure. He discovered that it had not displaced the same amount of water but a lesser amount, so that an ingot of gold has

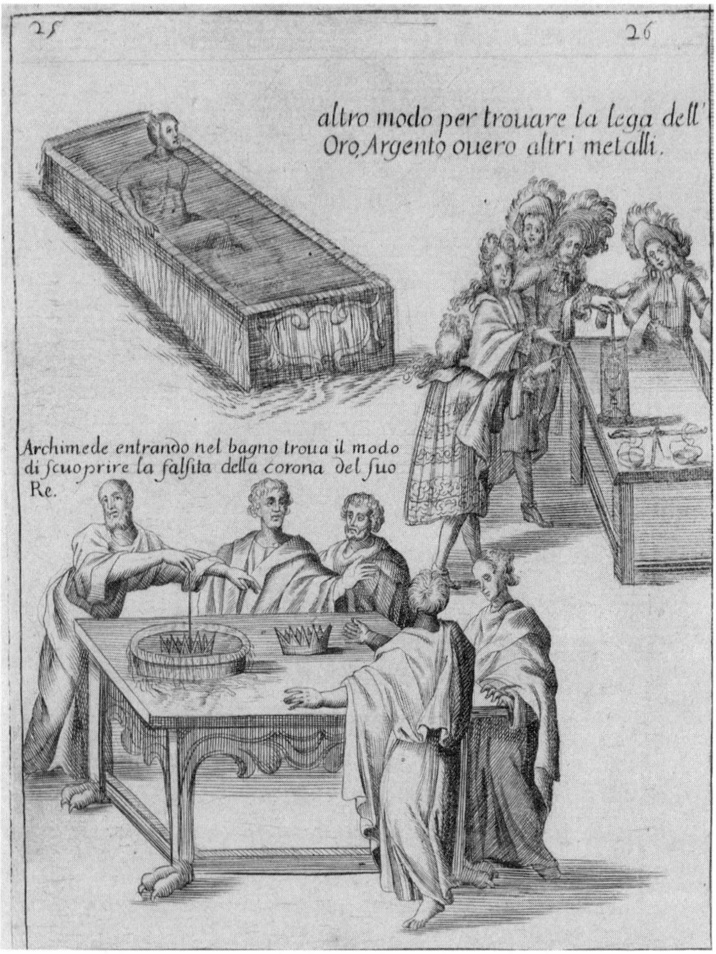

FIGURE 11

*The "Bath of Archimedes" and the method the scientist used to
discover whether the crown of Hiero was pure gold.
The engraving above is that of Cornelis Meyer from the volume entitled*
Nuovi Ritrovamenti *(Komarek, Rome, 1696), plate 6.*

FIGURE 12

*Archimedes, having placed the crown of Hiero on the ground,
puts in front of him two equal masses of gold and silver. (From an
engraving at f. 85v of the first illustrated edition of Vitruvius' De
architectura, published by Fra Giocondo in Venice in 1511.) In the
passage of Vitruvius, discussed on p. 33, two ingots, placed opposite
one another, are of the same weight but not of the same volume.*

less volume than a silver one of the same weight [in fact, the specific weight of gold is much greater than that of silver]. Then, having refilled the container and allowed the crown itself to drop into the same water, he found that the crown had displaced more water than did the mass of gold of the same weight. Thus, by developing an argument from the fact that more water was missing in the case of the crown than in the case of the gold ingot, he proved the presence of the silver alloy in the crown, thereby determining the metalworker's thievery. [*De architectura* 9, *pref.* 11–12; cf. fig. 12]

The specific weight of the crown was approximately between that of gold and silver; thus, from the act of immersion and from the cry "*Eureka!*" as well as from the denunciation of the metalworker's fraud, comes a more general scientific observation known as "Archimedes' principle." It states that a body heavier than the liquid in which it is immersed will descend to the bottom, but its weight in liquid will diminish the total weight of the container by as much as the volume of liquid displaced.[5] Another way of stating this would be: any object, wholly or partially immersed in a fluid, is buoyed up by a force equal to the weight of the fluid displaced by the object.

To put it in the simplest terms,

let it be supposed that solid volumes that are within the liquid are borne upwards and are driven in a vertical motion by their center of gravity.[6]

Though there are some differences, the similarities between the lively story of "*Eureka*" and the analysis that Archimedes makes of the problem in his treatise are striking, as the "excitement of discovery is replaced by the cool logic of geometrical demonstration."[7] In this regard, book 1, proposition 2 of *On Floating Bodies* seems particularly interesting, for in it Archimedes shows that "the surface of any undisturbed liquid will have the shape of a sphere, with the same center as the center of the earth," which also provides an explanation for the spherical shape of the surface of the earth's oceans.

V

ARCHIMEDES' MAGNUM OPUS
ON THE SPHERE AND THE CYLINDER

On the Sphere and the Cylinder is Archimedes' most extensive and well-argued scientific work that has come down to us. This work is concerned with geometric shapes that are not confined simply to flat surfaces, such as the sphere and the cylinder [plate 10a]. The ancients link the image of the Syracusan scientist to these shapes both through this work and, tangibly, through Archimedes' tomb, on which there were two precisely carved geometric figures, mentioned by Cicero (*Tusculan Disputations* 5, 64–66, cited more fully in chap. 10).

Other works of Archimedes, too, that have survived reveal themselves to have been driven by the question of measuring curvilinear shapes (such as spirals, parabolas, conoids, and spheroids). Admittedly, these objects are theoretical and encompass symbolic meanings: the circle and the sphere had particular mathematical and philosophical significance, as Netz has noted, linked to their roles in the various cosmologies of antiquity.[1] The treatise of

Archimedes includes some theorems on the volume of the cone and pyramid already outlined by Democritus at the end of the fifth century BC and, in the fourth century, demonstrated by Eudoxus: "each pyramid is the third part of the prism having an equal base and equal height, and each cone is the third part of the cylinder having equal base and equal height" (preface to *On the Sphere and the Cylinder*).

But Archimedes was able to enrich these theorems with "infinitesimal" arguments which specifically analyze solid figures by breaking them down into lines and circles of extreme thinness or, in the case of disproving a thesis, *argumentum ad absurdum*, which shows the inaccuracy of a hypothesis by bringing it to an absurd, even "meaningless," conclusion. By his infinitesimal argument, he was able to push his calculations to such a degree as to specify rather precisely the area and the volume of the sphere, the area of a section of the parabola, and the volume of the paraboloid as it spins. He was also able to identify their respective centers of gravity.

Archimedes gave some attention as well to ellipsoids and paraboloids in rotation, in his *On Conoids and Spheroids*, which was dedicated to the Alexandrian astronomer Dositheus. This treatise was one of the most original and mature works in Archimedes' corpus. In this work, which begins with complicated terms, Archimedes imagines and measures objects, in effect, far from daily experience. It treats solids obtained by performing a complete rotation of a flat curve around a fixed axis.

In particular:

- the elliptic paraboloid is achieved by rotating a parabola around its axis [fig. 13];
- the hyperboloid of two sheets is achieved by rotating a hyperbola around its transverse axis [fig. 14];
- the spheroid is achieved by the rotation of an ellipse (Archimedes distinguishes between a flattened

spheroid and an elongated spheroid, depending on whether the rotation takes place around the greater or lesser axis) [fig. 15].

As we said at the end of chapter 2, conic sections are curves described by the intersection of a cone with different planes:

- if the plane is parallel to one of the generators of the cone, it is considered a parabola.
- if the plane intersects both halves of a right circular cone at an angle parallel to the axis of the cone, it is considered a hyperbola;
- if the plane is not parallel to the axis, base, or generators of the cone, it is considered an ellipse;
- if the plane is perpendicular to the axis of the cone, it is considered a circle.

In addition to determining their volume, Archimedes also established the notion of segments of conoids and spheroids, i.e., of the parts of these shapes when limited by a plane.

Archimedes' work *On the Sphere and the Cylinder* should be considered as an ideal continuation of Euclid's *Elements*, published a few decades earlier, in which the main results of Greek mathematics were presented in a strictly deductive manner. That work did not treat the sphere, a solid shape that is considered more relevant to astronomy than geometry, in a comprehensive fashion. Indeed, whereas the *Elements* of Euclid is an amalgam of the results and previous knowledge of different authors, the work of Archimedes is almost completely original. *On the Sphere and the Cylinder* is divided into two books, which may have originally been two separate publications. The first book considers the measurement of surface area and volume of the sphere and its various sectors, while the second outlines a number of problems that are presented in producing and in dividing a sphere according to precise

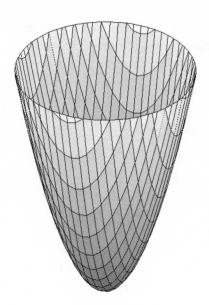

FIGURE 13

An elliptic paraboloid obtained by rotating a parabola.

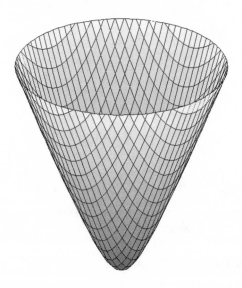

FIGURE 14

One half of a hyperboloid of two sheets obtained by rotating a hyperbola.

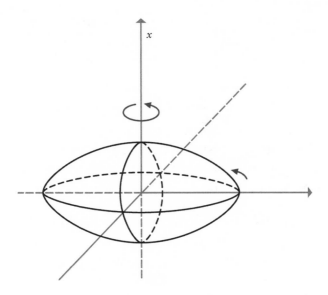

FIGURE 15

A spheroid in rotation around an X-axis.

---

parameters. These two books, as well as *Measurement of a Circle* and *On the Equilibrium of Planes*, garnered critical attention even in antiquity, as revealed in the sizable commentaries of Eutocius, which have been preserved in the manuscript tradition. Eutocius was one of the greatest mathematicians of late antiquity, born at the beginning of the sixth century AD at Ascalon in Palestine. His commentaries are full of information about the history of mathematics, among which are fragments of letters with requests for information exchanged between Archimedes and leading scientists of his own time who resided in Alexandria.

On the Sphere and the Cylinder introduced new concepts, such as "concavity" (in the definitions for book I), and some very important premises, including the claim that

> the smallest distance between all lines with the same extremes is a straight line,

that is to say, "the shortest distance between two points is a straight line" (the first premise).

The fifth premise is also especially significant. Since the second half of the nineteenth century, this famous premise has commonly been referred to as the postulate of Archimedes and is the basis of the theory of relations between magnitudes. It states that given two magnitudes (A and B) that belong to the same class, and assuming that A is greater than B, there is a multiple of the difference between A and B (A – B) which exceeds any other magnitude C homogenous with the first two.[2]

Archimedes is successful in establishing the principles that link the sphere with the cylinder and the cone, of which the most important are:

- the surface of any sphere is quadruple the largest circle it can contain (book I, proposition 33, with modern formula $S = 4r^2$);
- every sphere is 4 times the cone whose base equals the sphere's maximum circumference, and whose height is the radius of the sphere [fig. 16] (book I, proposition 34, with modern expression $S = {}^4/_3 r^3$).

And with its respective corollary, which served to give the title to the whole:

> Every cylinder having as its base the sphere's maximum circumference, and having a height equal to the diameter of the sphere, is one and a half times the sphere, and its surface, including its bases, is one and a half times the surface of the sphere [fig. 17].

FIGURE 16

The volume of a sphere is four times the volume of the cone that has as a base the maximum circle and as a height the radius of the sphere.

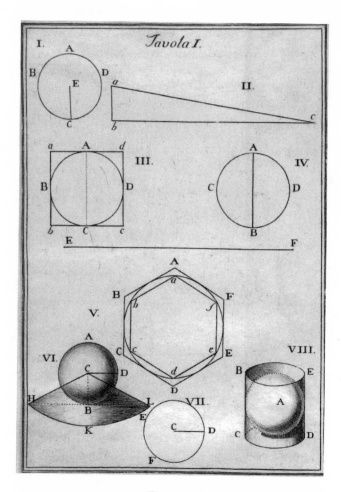

FIGURE 17

A drawing from Notizie istoriche e critiche intorno alla vita, alle invenzioni ed agli scritti di Archimede Siracusano *by Gian Maria Mazzucchelli (Brescia: Rizzardi, 1737). In the drawing, figures I and II represent the equivalency between the circle and the triangle, and a rectangle that has the circle's radius for its height and its circumference for its base. Figure VI reveals that the sphere is equivalent to the cone that has for its base the surface of the sphere and its radius for its height. In figure VIII the sphere is inscribed in a cylinder that has for its base the circumference of the circle and for its height the diameter; its volume and surface are ²/₃ of those of the cylinder.*

As Reviel Netz observes:

> The surface of the sphere is a two-dimensional object that
> is located in three-dimensional space and at no point is
> flat. The fact that it is equal to a simple two-dimensional
> object—four times the maximum circumference—is a
> kind of reduction in the size of the curvature: if the sur-
> faces of the spheres can be reduced to circles, the world
> is, in a sense, less curved. What makes this reduction
> even more satisfying is that the object that allows the
> reduction, the sphere, and that by which it comes to be
> reduced, the circle, are present in each other. Moreover,
> the numerical relationship that exists between them is
> very simple.[3]

Archimedes gave a great deal of attention to solid
rhombuses, formed by two cones with the same bases, and
vertices coming from the opposite side (but not necessarily
at the same height) with axes on the same line (definition
6). He expressed personal astonishment at the fact that different bodies with noteworthy characteristics were ignored
for a very long time:

> In fact, although these properties were always inherent
> in the nature of the figures, and although many excel-
> lent geometricians had flourished before Eudoxus, these
> remained universally unknown, and no one included
> them in treatises.[4]

At the end of the first book, and especially in the
second book of *On the Sphere and the Cylinder*, Archimedes extends his measuring even to sectors and spherical
segments, showing inter alia that

> for any spherical sector there exists an equal cone having
> a base that is equal to the surface of the spherical seg-
> ment relative to the sector, with its height equal to the
> radius of the sphere. [book I, proposition 44]

The argument is freewheeling and brilliant, and one gets the impression of moving, as Netz has said, "around the sphere as if in a dream," an amazing feat both from an aesthetic and from a mathematical point of view.

Archimedes uses another letter to Dositheus to open the second book of the treatise, where the Syracusan scientist confronts a series of rather complex problems. The first of them is the search for a sphere equivalent to a cone or a cylinder (proposition 1), a proportional measurement that Archimedes obtains through the study of the average proportion between two segments. This discovery leads Eutocius to make a large digression on the various solutions devised by the Greek mathematicians to solve the problem of doubling of the cube (his commentary on the second book has a triple extension in respect to Archimedes' original).

A solution to the problem was proposed by the Pythagorean Archytas in the first half of the fourth century BC, and other solutions, too, very different from those of the Syracusan scientist, were discovered in the centuries that followed. Eutocius describes twelve such solutions, and he also furnishes for us in this context a sizable fragment of Erotasthenes.[5]

In the second book, Archimedes also deals with the search for a spherical segment similar to another and equivalent to a third (proposition 5) and, in the end, proves the theorem (proposition 9):

> Among all the spherical segments comprised of equal surface area [and belonging to different spheres], the greatest is the hemisphere.

Archimedes' work leads to a fundamental innovation in both research methods and geometric concepts and has constituted an important basis for future developments in mathematics and geometry, from ancient times, through the Renaissance, to the modern age. Arabic sources also mention a treatise entitled *On the Construction of the Sphere*, in which the Syracusan scientist would have given the necessary instructions to make a planetarium of the kind brought to Rome as the spoils of war by the general Marcellus (see end of chap. 1).

HOW MANY GRAINS OF SAND DOES IT TAKE TO FILL THE UNIVERSE?

In his short treatise entitled *The Sand Reckoner*, Archimedes proposes to count the grains of sand contained in a sphere that has the sun at its center and has the sky as its periphery, demarcated by fixed stars. To this end, Archimedes had to devise a numbering system capable of expressing very large numbers in some way equivalent to our binary calculus or, in fact, closer to what we call exponential notation [fig. 18]. He came to the following conclusion:

> It is clear therefore that the fullness of sand, having its volume equal to the sphere of fixed stars, as Aristarchus hypothesizes, is less than 1,000 thousands of the 8th order of numbers.[1] And these, O King Gelon, I understand not to appear to be easily accepted by the rabble who have no familiarity with calculations, but rather by those who have considered the distances and sizes of the earth and the sun and the moon and the entire cosmos, that they may regard them as believable on account of

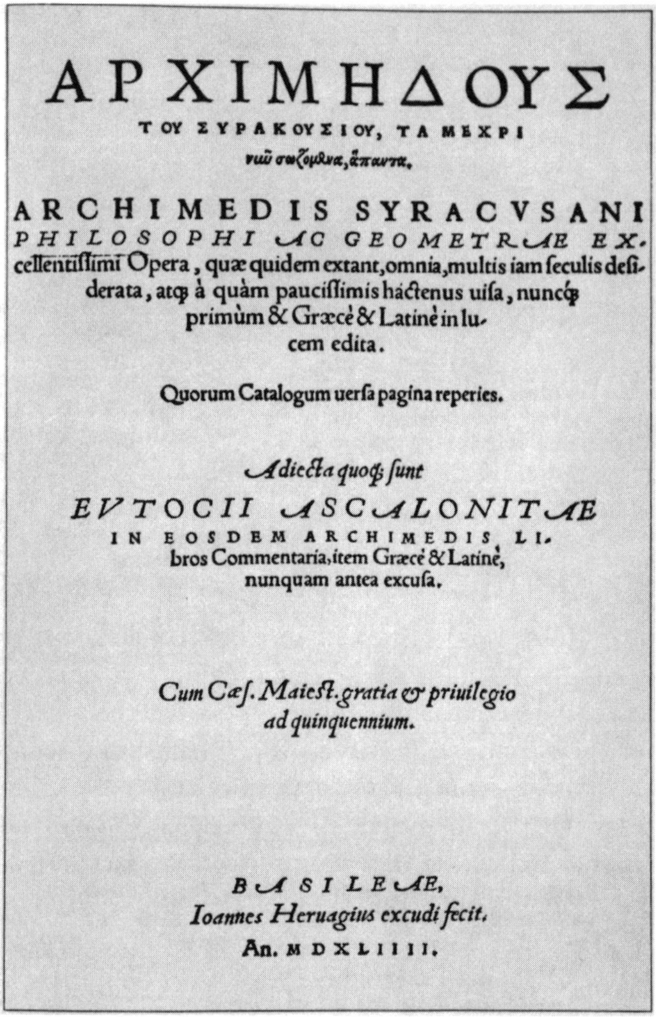

ΑΡΧΙΜΗΔΟΥΣ
T OY ΣΥΡΑΚΟΥΣΙΟΥ, ΤΑ ΜΕΧΡΙ
νῦν σωζόμενα, ἅπαντα.

ARCHIMEDIS SYRACVSANI
PHILOSOPHI AC GEOMETRAE EX-
cellentiſſimi Opera, quæ quidem extant, omnia, multis iam ſeculis deſi-
derata, atq̃ à quàm pauciſſimis hàctenus uiſa, nunc̃q
primùm & Græcè & Latinè in lu-
cem edita.

Quorum Catalogum uerſa pagina reperies.

Adiecta quoq̃ ſunt
EVTOCII ASCALONITAE
IN EOSDEM ARCHIMEDIS, LI-
bros Commentaria, item Græcè & Latinè,
nunquam antea excuſa.

Cum Cæſ. Maieſt. gratia & priuilegio
ad quinquennium.

BASILEAE,
Ioannes Heruagius excudi fecit.
An. M DXLIIII.

FIGURE 18

*Frontispiece of the first modern edition of Archimedes, published
at Basel in 1544. It represents the Greek text of both works of
Archimedes known up to that time, including the late antique
commentary of Eutocius and a complete Latin translation. Thereafter
the base of readers of Archimedes throughout Europe would expand
and, within a few years, would form a daringly innovative scientific
community.*

my demonstration. Therefore I thought that it would not
be inappropriate for you to consider these things.

Unlike his other works, this one is not dedicated to a
scientist but to a ruler of Syracuse, with whom Archimedes
clearly enjoyed a good deal of familiarity. This work turns
out to be quite different in terms of style and content, and,
in terms of its goal, it catches the reader off guard, virtually
disorienting him with "a style of suspense and surprise."[2]

To that end, if the problem ostensibly was to calculate
the number of grains of sand necessary to fill the entire
universe, Archimedes chiefly must have sought to calculate its size in terms of space. As Dijksterhuis has noted,
"The work *The Sand-Reckoner,* though meant by the
author as a contribution to Greek arithmetic, owes its historical interest not only to what it contains as such; it is no
less valuable as a document of Archimedes' astronomical
activity. It was of course to be expected that he engaged
in astronomy, though he has not left any work exclusively
devoted to it: astronomy and mathematics in his day were
scarcely distinguished as two different branches of science."[3]

It is interesting how, at the opening of *The Sand Reckoner*, Archimedes gives the measurement, essentially cor-
rect, even if done with simple means, of the angle according
to which the sun is visible in the sky (between 32 and 27
sixtieths of a degree):

> The diameter of the sun is approximately 30 times
> greater than the diameter of the moon and not more . . .
> in addition, the diameter of the sun is greater than the
> side of a thousand-sided polygon inscribed on the big-
> gest circle that the cosmos could possibly contain.

This calculation is rendered by means of optics, a science which forms a bridge between geometry and astronomy. In his demonstration, Archimedes explicitly refers

to Aristarchus, the astronomer who, at the beginning of the third century BC, first formulated the hypothesis for the heliocentric solar system[4] and had found that the sun occupies approximately the seven hundred and twentieth part of the circle of the zodiac.

The Sand Reckoner also reveals the autobiographical detail that Archimedes' father had worked specifically on astronomy. In addition, from *The Sand Reckoner* we learn about the practical tools used for these calculations, i.e., the straight edge and a sliding cylinder:

> When the sun is almost on the horizon and is able to be observed, a straight edge is turned toward the sun, and one places one's eye at the flat of the straight edge. Then a cylinder, placed between the sun and one's eye, obscures the sun. The cylinder is then moved little by little away from one's eye, ending where a sliver of the sun begins to appear at both ends of the cylinder.

Thus he describes the instrument which seems to have been used to calculate the diameters of the sun and the moon, as well as the angle by which their diameters can be seen from earth, resulting in a measurement remarkably accurate for the period in which Archimedes lived.

Archimedes never disdained unusual or even trivial questions. To his taste for mathematical games one can attribute at least two short but significant works, perhaps composed in his youth: *The Stomachion* and *The Cattle Problem*.[5]

Of *The Stomachion*, a few passages have come down to us in an Arabic translation, while others have survived in Greek. These Greek verses were preserved in a palimpsest entitled *The Method on Mechanical Theorems* (see chap. 8). *Stomachion* was the name of a game, somewhat similar to a puzzle—perhaps already in use before Archimedes—that was designed to stimulate children's intelligence and to test their ability to think and imagine, thus encouraging their creativity. It consisted of fourteen ivory tiles variously but proportionately cut to form a square;[6] the pieces had the form of scalene and isosceles triangles, squares, and other polygons. With imagination and repetition, the pieces could compose numerous figures: an enormous elephant, a wild boar, a flying goose, a hunter at his post, a dog barking, a tower, and many other images of this sort, varying in accordance with the dexterity of the player [plate 6].

Thus Ausonius, who lived in Gaul in the fourth century AD and whose poetry frequently alluded to some passages of late Latin grammarians and scholars, writes in his most famous work, the *Cento Nuptialis*,[7] that this game is called the *Loculus Archimedius*. We do not know how *The Stomachion* arrived in China, in either the ancient or medieval periods, or how it returned to Europe from there in the second half of the ninth century with the name Tangram, or "the Chinese Game" (but consisting of seven instead of fourteen pieces). Regardless, the scientific importance of this small work of Archimedes lies in the fact that the Syracusan mathematician was not focusing only on the possibility of creating different shapes, but also on the manner in which various combinations of the pieces could produce the same figure. This game therefore embodied a kind of refined puzzle within the realm of combinatorial geometry.[8]

The Cattle Problem is a treatise that expresses with sardonic wit an arithmetical problem. It is written in elegiac couplets cast in the form of epigrams to the geographer Eratosthenes of Alexandria. (The scientists of that time were also often poets of culture and good taste.) The work is not included in the transmitted collections of other works of Archimedes, having been discovered in 1773 in a manuscript at Wolfenbüttel by Gotthold Ephraim Lessing, the author of the famous philosophical treatise *Laocoon*. It represents the problem with eight variables, to be used for the precise calculation of the number of "the Cattle of the

Sun" that graze in the plains of Sicily. This herd is divided in a precise manner between bulls and cows, and likewise among those that are white, black, mottled, and tawny. The precise constituency of the herd must satisfy a series of mathematical proportions:

- white bulls are equal to a half plus one third more of black bulls, in addition to all the tawny: $W = (\frac{1}{2} + \frac{1}{3})B + T$;
- black bulls are equal to one fourth plus one fifth of all the mottled, in addition to all the tawny: $B = (\frac{1}{4} + \frac{1}{5})M + T$;
- the remaining mottled are equivalent to the sixth part plus one seventh of the white bulls, plus all the tawny: $M = (\frac{1}{6} + \frac{1}{7})W + T$.

There were yet more complicated conditions beyond these, as well. After having established these quantities, and after having demonstrated all sizes of numbers, he could boast to have been the one person who solved the conundrum and who would thus be esteemed for such an erudite calculation.

One might go so far as to compare the winner of this mathematical "contest" to a victorious athlete. Yet we do not know whether Eratosthenes of Alexandria or some other scientist in antiquity actually solved the problem. In the algebraic language of today, the cattle problem is translated into a system of equations with eight variables. The minimum solution obtainable from these equations, which then measures the total number of animals of the herds of the sun (as the German mathematician Amthor proved in 1880), is 7,766 followed by 206,541 zeros. Thus, it is a number so large and complex that it gives cause for doubt as to whether Archimedes or Eratosthenes, to whom the poem was dedicated, could really have solved the riddle. Although, as *The Sand Reckoner* attests, Archimedes undoubtedly had the capacity to conceive of huge numbers, there is no evidence that he actually used such mastery to succeed in performing this particular calculation, remaining faithful to all the conditions of the problem that he had himself laid out.

ARCHIMEDES AS CIVIL AND MILITARY ENGINEER

Of all the machines constructed under Archimedes' direction, the ship *Syracusia*, ordered by the tyrant Hiero II in 240 BC as a token of the tyrant's prosperous reign, occupies a special place. It was, in all likelihood, the largest vessel of antiquity, with a vast capacity estimated between 3,650 and 4,200 tons,[1] a capability that would not be seen again until the nineteenth century, when iron and steel, in particular, were introduced for the construction of holds [plate 7].

A fascinating description of the *Syracusia* has been handed down by the third-century AD author Athenaeus in the *Deipnosophistae* ("Professors at Dinner"),[2] a work that has only recently begun to receive adequate scholarly attention. It is preserved in a tenth-century codex of the Biblioteca Marciana in Venice, recopied many times from that source during the Renaissance. Athenaeus reports that Archimedes imagined a complex system of winches and pulleys that would allow only a few men to launch the huge boat in the sea or carry it on land [fig. 19; plate 8].

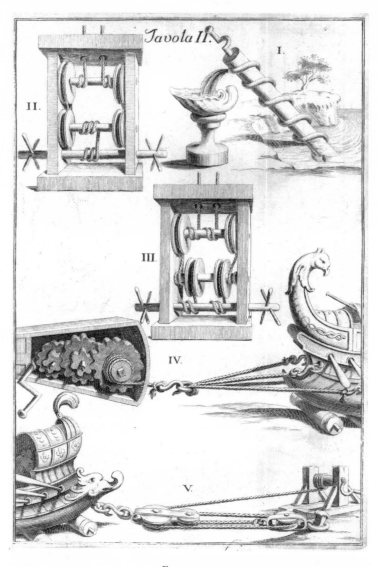

FIGURE 19

System of winches and pulleys (also known as Archimedes' block and tackle) invented to move with little effort even very large weights, such as the ship Syracusia, *here depicted in a reconstruction by Gian Maria Mazzucchelli in a drawing from his biography of Archimedes (Brescia: Rizzardi, 1737).*

Moreover, Athenaeus reports that Archimedes carried out the scientific and technical supervision of the undertaking of the building of the ship. Upon its completion, the *Syracusia* was offered as a gift to the Egyptian rulers of Alexandria by the Syracusans, providing a tangible symbol of both the Sicilian city's wealth and political sway. In a gesture suited to the occasion, Hiero changed the name of the boat to *Alexandris*.

To keep the ship's hold dry, Archimedes designed a large bilge pump known as the *cochlea* ("snail"), sometimes referred to as the "the screw of Archimedes." This instrument, brilliant in its simplicity, was a spiral siphon consisting of a vine-like spiral running inside a cylinder with a crank that could be operated by a single sailor, possibly by foot power. The water entered from the base, itself lower than the inclined vine-like spiral, making its way upward by the revolutions of the spiral; the flow of water was continuous, so that it did not leave any more unwanted residue than had the older laborious system of buckets [plate 9]. The height to which water could be raised would have depended on the length and inclination of the device. That this kind of spiral pump could be used for industry is mentioned also by the first-century BC historian Diodorus Siculus, who describes how such a machine was used in a Spanish mine:

> Sometimes, deep in the earth, miners break into subterranean rivers, whose force they overcome by cutting through their supply streams with crooked ditches as those streams cascade into the rivers. Driven by the promise of gain . . . the miners draw off the streams by so-called Egyptian screws, which Archimedes of Syracuse discovered when he visited Egypt. And because of these screws, the men are continually able to transport the water up to the mine's opening through a kind of a

relay device, thereby drying up the area for mining and readying it for use. [*Historical Library* 5.37]

Some parts of large snail-like screws from the Roman period have been found in a mine in Spain in the province of Huelva, near the coast, due west of Seville [fig. 20]. These pumps would have been of such size that a single one of them could raise the water from the bottom of a well to a height of about 10 meters. The calculations were made by modern scholars following the instructions of Vitruvius outlined in *De architectura* (10.6). It has been calculated that the screw could pump, for each single meter, about 200 liters of water per minute (cf. fig. 21).[3]

Some historians of science, however, suspect that an apparatus similar to that of Archimedes was already in use, which merely came to his notice in 243 BC during his journey in Egypt, where the instrument might have been used to pump water to irrigate the fields not directly flooded by the Nile. The verb "discovered" in Diodorus' account (cited above) is as ambiguous in Greek as it is in English. If this verb means "came across," then Archimedes would only have been responsible for the perfection of this instrument.[4] Nevertheless, while before Archimedes' time a vast quantity of iconographic material related to the labors necessary for the regulation of the Nile's propensity to flood certainly did come from Egypt, no image depicting a device resembling the snail-spiral has been found. The Roman architectural writer Vitruvius, though he does not explicitly associate Archimedes with the spiral, concludes his description of the device by showing how this fairly simple instrument produced significant results [cf. plate 16]:

> I have fully explained, as clearly as I could, about the wooden apparatus constructed at that time to draw water, describing the techniques used to accomplish this and some of the factors by which the devices are set

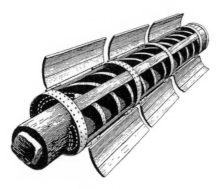

FIGURE 20

A modern drawing of the screw of Archimedes, constructed out of oak wood, based on the type found in Spain.

FIGURE 21

A drawing depicting how the screw of Archimedes functioned, taken from a woodcut of f. 102r in the illustrated edition of Vitruvius published in Venice in 1511.

in motion, establishing with their rotations an unlimited quantity of practical applications. [*De architectura* 10.6.6]

Archimedes' engineering accomplishments also extended to the political and specifically military concerns of his home town of Syracuse. Linked by kinship and political alliance with the tyrant Hiero II and Hiero's young nephew Hieronymus (who succeeded him fifteen years later in 215 BC, shortly after the terrible Roman defeat at Cannae), Archimedes was convinced by the elders of Syracuse

to devote some of his skill in theoretical knowledge to concrete things and apply his method of inquiry to material needs, so as to make it more obvious to the layman and . . . to devise both defensive and offensive weaponry, which could be of use in any type of siege. [*Life of Marcellus* 14]

The third-century AD Greek biographer Plutarch continues, describing Archimedes as convinced that

the practice of making of machines, like any other art that addresses immediate utility, was ignoble and merely mechanical. He thus turned his attention exclusively to more ambitious studies, the beauty and abstraction of which are untainted by ordinary material needs. [*Life of Marcellus* 18]

Thus Plutarch tells us, if a bit fancifully, that during the siege of Syracuse by the Roman general Marcus Claudius Marcellus, between 213 and 212 BC, "his device served the needs of the Syracusans" (*Life of Marcellus* 14). Plutarch continues,

[Marcellus commanded] a fleet of sixty quinqueremes filled with all kinds of arms and projectiles. And on a great platform consisting of eight ships fastened together, Marcellus had built a launching machine aimed in the

direction of the walls, confident in the size and splen-
dor of the device as well as in the fame that surrounded
him. But Archimedes was not at all concerned with any
of this, as if the enemies' weapons paled in comparison
with his own mechanisms. [*Life of Marcellus* 14]

Within two generations of those events, the Greek historian Polybius, in his now fragmentary eighth book, wrote
about this same "technological war":

Having prepared their wicker shields, bolts, and other
siege weapons, the Romans expected to outstrip the enemy's preparations within five days, thanks to the many
arms they had for the undertaking. They did not, however, have proper regard for the aptitude of Archimedes,
nor did they have the foresight to realize that in certain
circumstances a single mind is more effective than any
number of arms. Still, they came to know the truth of
this through experience. [*The Histories* 8.3.3]

In particular, Archimedes promoted the use of huge and
accurate catapults that he had created [plate 11]:

When they saw the Romans besieging the city on two
fronts, land and sea, the Syracusans were stunned and
fell silent from fear. For they supposed that nothing
could resist such force and might. But once Archimedes let loose his machines, arrows of every kind rained
down upon the enemy infantry. Great masses of rock
were also flung from on high with noise and incredible
speed. And since no one could defend himself from their
impact, the stones were knocking over all those whom
they struck and were disrupting the ranks . . . With
regard to the war machine that Marcellus was carrying
on his platform . . . as it approached the wall from a
great distance, a stone weighing ten talents flew out at
it, followed by a second and then a third. Some projectiles, as they struck the machine clamorously, created a

> billowing wave, and destroyed the machine's foundation
> by shattering its connection to its base and separating it
> from the platform. [*Life of Marcellus* 15][5]

Some questions remain concerning the use of other magnificent machines of which the ancients make mention, such as

> Beams being extended suddenly from the wall over the
> ships sank some, plunging them into the depths by drop-
> ping weights on them, while others were picked up by an
> iron claw or by a "beak" similar to that of a crane, and
> were then immersed stern-first into the water. [*Life of
> Marcellus* 14;[6] cf. plate 12]

Not so secure, however, is the ancient attestation to the "burning mirrors," which were supposedly used by Archimedes to focus sunlight and ignite the ships of Marcellus from a distance; indeed, historians of science have remained skeptical as to the existence of such a device [plate 13]. One does, however, perhaps find a reference to this mechanism in the oration "On Magic" (chap. 16) spoken by the African writer Apuleius in the second century AD,[7] and in one of the dialogues of Lucian (53.2). The two Byzantine historians Zonaras and Tzetzes, however, speak explicitly of it only in the twelfth century, when they state precisely that the ingenious Syracusan scientist would have used hexagonal mirrors [fig. 22].[8] There is, too, a passage in Galen's *De temperamentis* (*On Temperaments* 93.16[9]), which occurs also in Arabic editions and in Renaissance translators, that reinterprets the "burning mirrors" (*speculis ardentibus*) as actually referring to pouring boiling pitch from the defensive wall upon the attacking enemies (cf. fig. 23).[10]

FIGURE 22

Archimedes holding in his hand one of his "burning mirrors."
The sculpture was made by Giuseppe Villa in 1870 and is now in the
lobby of the Orso Mario Corbino Scientific High School in Syracuse,
Italy. It is possible that Archimedes never actually used these mirrors
but merely designed them, having discovered that rays reflected from
parabolic mirrors converge on a single point, which is not the case
with spherical mirrors.

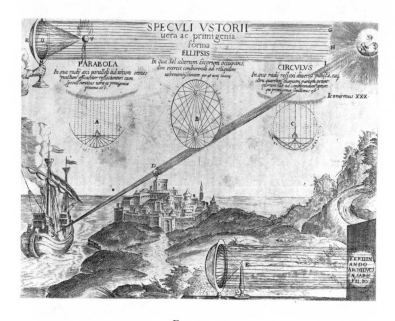

FIGURE 23

*The presumed operation of the burning mirrors in a reconstruction
by the erudite German Athanasius Kircher in a drawing on p. 883
of his* Ars Magna Lucis et Umbrae *(Rome: Ludovico Grignani, 1646).*

AN ORIGINAL AND PERSUASIVE METHOD

Archimedes' short work entitled *The Method on Mechanical Theorems* has had a stormy history. Lost for many centuries, it was rediscovered by chance in a manuscript that arrived in Istanbul from Jerusalem's Monastery of the Holy Sepulcher in 1906. The work was quickly translated into German and published in 1907 by its discoverer, the Danish philologist Johan Ludvig Heiberg. In that same year a large commentary on Archimedes' work appeared, written by Hieronymus Georg Zeuthen, a historian of mathematics.

Just after the First World War, however, the codex disappeared, probably stolen from Munich during a transfer of manuscripts from the Istanbul headquarters of the Orthodox Patriarchate of Jerusalem at the National Library of Athens. Fortunately, this manuscript was rediscovered at the end of the last century; it was put to auction on 29 October 1998 at Christie's in New York, fetching the remarkable figure of $2,150,000. The new owner, an

American billionaire, has entrusted the document for safe-keeping to the Walters Art Museum in Baltimore, while 1906 photographs of Heiberg, the manuscript's discoverer, now faded, are housed in the Royal Library in Copenhagen, Denmark.

The Method of Mechanical Theorems is contained in a palimpsest. This document consists of the codex containing Archimedes' ancient text, copied afresh in the tenth century, which, about two hundred years later, was expunged and rewritten with a series of prayers and Christian texts.[1] Aside from the many portions of works already known to have belonged to Archimedes, which it often also manages to integrate—these works include *On Floating Bodies*, which had been known up to that time only in a medieval Latin translation—the manuscript has enabled us to acquaint ourselves with almost the entire text devoted explicitly to the *Method*, hitherto lost. This discovery is truly one of the greatest moments in the entire history of mathematics [plate 14].

This brief treatise is more dialogic than the greater part of the scientific treatises of Greek mathematics passed down to us. The work itself is presented as if a letter to Archimedes' contemporary Eratosthenes, mathematician, astronomer, geographer, and poet, who was at that time director of the Museum at Alexandria:

> Seeing that you are a diligent and excellent teacher of philosophy, and also given that it is a great thing to appreciate in mathematics the theory that falls to your consideration, I decided to write to you and express in this same book the characteristics of a certain method, through which you will be given the opportunity to address mathematical issues through mechanical means. And I am convinced that this method is no less useful for the demonstration of these purely mathematical theorems. In fact some of the properties that I have first

presented by mechanics were later proven to me through geometry, since the research carried out by means of this method is not really a demonstration. For, since this method has already obtained some knowledge of what you seek, it is easier to complete the demonstration after mechanical research than to press on in research without any prior understanding. [Praefatio, *Method*]

In reaching his findings, together with mathematical procedures of the infinitesimal type[2] Archimedes uses, in a distinctly original way, arguments about mechanics, which he denies have absolute value. These arguments, however, have value for imagining and producing new discoveries. Thus Archimedes anticipates his mathematical successors:

I am confident that some mathematicians present or future, having been shown this method, will find other theorems not yet imagined by us. [Praefatio, *Method*]

The *geometric method* was used only at a later time to demonstrate rigorously propositions already identified as a mechanically plausible [fig. 24].

The exposition of Archimedes is of great interest, as Lucio Russo has noted, for someone who is trying to communicate not only the proofs of his results but also the mental route that led to them.[3]

From a philosophical point of view, it is possible to consider the application of mathematics to physics as a necessary corollary, owing to the abstract and general nature of mathematics, but the reverse attribution is far more problematic. For example, one cannot say that the behavior of a lever could influence the natural properties of a line, a triangle, or a parabola.

Practically speaking, then, Archimedes' *Method* consisted of the application of mechanical arguments to produce mathematical innovations. Though he presents them

FIGURE 24

Corner rulers and compasses found at Pompeii.

in a condensed fashion in his work, he notes that he will demonstrate them with geometric rigor later. Attilio Frajese has offered an eloquent comparison:

> We would say that this is a matter of "math behind the scenes": as if in a theater, at some point in the representation, the viewer, gets up from his seat in the audience and is led on stage, behind the scenes, that he may, with the new observation point, learn the secrets of the organization of the spectacle.[4]

Yet "behind the scenes" need not imply that Archimedes' quest for knowledge gave birth to one intuitive event after another, as the sense of discovery embodied in Archimedes' famous exaltation *"Eureka!"* would suggest (cf. chap. 4). Inasmuch as, with the passage of time, a discovery can only be corroborated or proved incorrect, it is significant that, in the preface to his *On Spirals*, Archimedes admits that he had passed on to Conon two false theorems, incompatible with others already demonstrated.

Conon, however, died before he could examine these theorems, and indeed no one had noticed their spuriousness before Archimedes himself revealed it, quipping ironically about the arrogance of colleagues in Alexandria:

> so that those who claim to be able to discover everything, without reporting any demonstration, are refuted because in fact they discovered impossible things. [Praefatio, *On Spirals*]

A particular result of the *Method* of Archimedes is the determination of the gravitational center not only of polygonal planes or simple shapes, but also of complex rotating shapes, such as spherical segments equal to or less than a hemisphere, segments of ellipsoid, paraboloids, and hyperboloids. Archimedes demonstrates such discoveries on several occasions. Though he imputes some value to mechanical deductions, he clearly puts greater weight on rigorous demonstration:

> As already it was to Aristotle, perhaps also for Archimedes the decisive question was finding premises adequate for the construction of the demonstration of results achieved by other means.[5]

ARCHIMEDES AND THE POETS CATULLUS, HORACE, AND VIRGIL

The innovations of Archimedes found their way into Latin poetry beginning, in all probability, with Ennius, whose eighth book of *Annales* described the Roman conquest of Sicily. Although unfortunately we only have about half of the verses of his description,[1] we do have Silius Italicus' account of the same conquest, composed approximately three centuries later. In the fourteenth book of his *Punica*, Silius portrays Archimedes as "defender of the fatherland" (*defensor patriae*, 676), mentioning, too, his innovative discoveries in weaponry (300–304) but chiefly celebrating the fact that through him the "heavens and earth were laid bare" (*caelum terraeque paterent*, 343), a reference to his discoveries in physics, meteorology, and astronomy.[2]

A year after Ennius' death in 168 BC, the Roman historian Polybius, who wrote in Greek, brought Archimedes to Rome as a hostage. In the fragmentary eighth book of his *Histories*, Polybius left us the first detailed account of how the scientist had undertaken the defense of Syracuse (*The Histories* 8.5–9).

Polybius established Archimedes' reputation among the Romans, a reputation that remained strong throughout the centuries. In the first century BC, for example, one could still admire the two splendid planetariums transferred to Rome as spoils of war many years earlier by the conqueror of Syracuse, Marcus Claudius Marcellus, who had one put in his own home and the other in the temple of Virtus. Cicero explains this story with a touch of *Schadenfreude*:

> [Sulpicius Gallus asked to see] a celestial globe, saved by Marcellus' grandfather after the capture of that most opulent and magnificent city, Syracuse. This alone was the spoil he brought home from so great a victory. I had often heard mention made of this celestial globe on account of the glorious reputation of Archimedes. I was not so much amazed, however, at its appearance alone, for there was yet another, more elegant and better known, fashioned by Archimedes, which that same Marcellus had deposited in the Temple of Virtus at Rome. [*De re publica* 1.21]

There are other noteworthy references to Archimedes in the Ciceronian corpus. In his *Tusculan Disputations* (5.23.64), for example, Cicero offers a moving account of how, when he was a financial officer (*quaestor*) in Sicily, he rediscovered Archimedes' tomb, having come across it in Syracuse. A sphere surrounding a cylinder was engraved on it, representing in plastic art the subject of Archimedes' celebrated mathematical work *On the Sphere and the Cylinder*.[3]

Cicero's account of the two suggests that the ancient orator appreciated Archimedes' theoretical contribution more than even the amazing machines that he designed for civilian or military use. Such recognition of Archimedes' acumen was not lost on Cicero's contemporary writers. In Latin poetry, in particular, Archimedes' fame has a distinctive flavor.

Such a reputation is not surprising, since the separation between scientific and humanistic culture was much less starkly defined than it is today, and the intellectuals of the time were trying to repeat at Rome the dialogue that earlier critics and poets had maintained with scientists in the museum at Alexandria.[4] Ennius, for example, had already treated subjects related to the properties of nature in a small poem entitled "Epicharmus," of which eight short fragments survive. For that poem's title he borrowed the name of the Sicilian poet of the Pythagorean tradition, who himself had written in a playful style on topics pertaining both to science and mythology.

Any explicit mention of Archimedes, however, posed a particular difficulty for poets, as the name of the scientist begins with a metrical unit known as a "cretic" (long–short–long). Qua sound, therefore, "Archimedes" could not be formulated within the hexameter verse that many poets, especially those who wrote epic or didactic verse, regularly employed. The Roman epicist Silius Italicus, for example, is thus unable to mention Archimedes by name, even though he expresses great admiration for his work in physics and mathematics and for his contributions to military science.

To obviate this metrical obstacle, in his third bucolic poem Virgil refers to Archimedes with a circumlocution that, by virtue of the manner of presentation, especially stands out. Through the banter of two characters, Virgil describes somewhat cryptically a cup offered as a prize for a poetic competition:

In medio duo signa, Conon et—quis fuit alter,
descripsit radio totum qui gentibus orbem,
tempora quae messor, quae curuos arator haberet?

Eclogues 3.40–42

[In the middle are two emblems, one of Conon, and the other—who was the other? Was it he who described the entire cosmos for humankind with a rod, explaining what seasons the reaper and what seasons the stooping plowman should have?]

These verses are in the learned style of Hellenistic poetry. Virgil refers first to Conon, who was born in Samos but resided in Alexandria, where he was an astronomer. Virgil's citation of his name in the *Eclogues* stands in the classical world as a sophisticated tribute to the bridge between science and poetry. Conon's reputation in literature was due mainly to Callimachus, who in his *Coma Berenices* had recounted how the queen of Egypt had hung her beautiful lock in a temple as an act of love for her husband Ptolemy Euergetes, when he had returned from war unharmed. Shortly after the lock had disappeared, Conon had explained the phenomenon by showing a new constellation in the sky, to which, as befit of a member of the royal court, he gave the name *The Lock of Berenice*.

Even more interesting, however, is Virgil's unanswered question that immediately follows: *quis fuit alter?* ["Who was the other?"] This question calls attention to the rusticity of the shepherd Menalcas, whose lapse in memory has drawn the attention of numerous scholars who have preoccupied themselves with his query. The most persuasive of the answers to Menalcas' question is found as early as the late-antique commentaries on the *Eclogues*, which identify the character as Archimedes. The author of the *Scholia Veronensia*, for example, writes on the passage *Nonnulli Archimedem* ("Some say Archimedes"), and a remark that has come down to us under the name of Probus is more pointed: "while it is uncertain who, after Conon, the "alterum" is, one might suspect Archimedes, inasmuch as he was Conon's student."[5] These early commentators answer Menalcas' question with Archimedes because of the fact that he had measured the diameter between sun and moon as well as the distance of both of these bodies from the earth. He also worked on the measurement of the earth's radius, and the Latin word *radius* (line 41 of Virgil's poem) signifies the "radius of a circle," which is one of the key points of Archimedes' mathematical works.

Just a few years before the *Eclogues,* Gaius Valerius Catullus, one of Virgil's important models, had himself imitated closely Callimachus' *The Lock of Berenice.* Catullus opened his sixty-sixth poem with a tribute to Zeno and his branch of learning (*Omnia qui magni dispexit lumina mundi,* "He who numbered the stars of the vast cosmos"). Catullus also had an interesting relationship with Cicero, whose work he knew well and to whom he had dedicated the drolly ironic poem 49 (*Dissertissime Romuli nepotum,* "Most witty of the grandchildren of Romulus"). In such a climate of rich intellectual and political interchange, it is not surprising that Catullus gives learned attention to large and small numbers in his fifth poem:[6]

> Da mi basia mille, deinde centum,
> dein mille altera, dein secunda centum,
> deinde usque altera mille, deinde centum;
> dein, cum milia multa fecerimus,
> conturbabimus illa, ne sciamus,
> aut ne quis malus inuidere possit,
> cum tantum sciat esse basiorum.

Catullus 5.7–13

[Give me a thousand kisses, then a hundred, then another thousand, then a second hundred, then even another thousand, then a hundred. Then, once we have given each other many a thousand kisses, we'll mix them all up, lest we know how many times we've kissed or lest any wicked person be able to look askance at us, even if he should know the great number of our kisses.]

One can find, perhaps, in this repeated series of numbers a reference to the calculating columns used for hundreds and thousands on an abacus, the handy instrument used by the Romans for reckoning large numbers.[7] One may well be able to see in these verses, too, a reference to Archimedes, who had put these numbers at the center of his highly original and, by Catullus' time, famous work, *The Sand Reckoner*. In addition, one finds a similar allusion to *The Sand Reckoner* in Catullus' seventh poem, where homage is paid to Callimachus by the specific recollection of that poet's birthplace, Cyrene (4):

Quaeris, quot mihi basiationes
tuae, Lesbia, sint satis superque.
Quam magnus numerus Libyssae arenae
lasarpiciferis iacet Cyrenis,
oraclum Iouis inter aestuosi
et Batti ueteris sacrum sepulcrum,
aut quam sidera multa, cum iacet nox,
furtiuos hominum uident amores,
tam te basia multa basiare
uesano satis et super Catullo est;
quae nec pernumerare curiosi
possint nec mala fascinare lingua.

Catullus 7.1–12

[You ask, Lesbia, how many of your kisses are enough and more than enough for me. The answer is as great as the number of grains of the sand of Libya that stretches out in silphium-bearing Cyrene, between the oracle of thirsty Jove and the sacred tomb of ancient Battus; or

how many stars, when the night is silent, look upon the
secret love affairs of human beings: enough and more
than enough for your crazy Catullus it is that you give
him so many kisses, which the curious are neither able
to count nor bewitch with an evil spell.]

Expressions such as "great number" (*magnus numerus,* 3) or "count" (*pernumerare,* 11) obviously belong to
mathematical language and, what is more, they clearly hark
back to Archimedes, who had contrasted the number of
grains of sand on the coast of Africa with the stars in the
cosmos. Catullus compares that vast number with the number of kisses that the poetic persona seeks from his lover.

The same image will return again in his so-called *Wed-
ding Poem* (poem 61), this time with a bold comparison
between the very large number of grains of sand and the
games of love that newlyweds play:

Ille pulueris Africi
siderumque micantium
subducat numerum prius,
qui uestri numerare uolt
multa milia ludi.

                                        61.206–10

[Let him reckon first the number of grains of African
sand or of shining stars, whoever wants to count the
many thousand aspects of your game (of love).]

Again, Archimedes is the historical persona who was
capable of this calculation, for he reckoned the grains of
sand, "not only those on the shore of Syracuse and the rest
of Sicily, but also of every coastline (inhabited or uninhab-
ited) of the earth and of the whole cosmos," as Archimedes vaunts at the opening of his *Sand Reckoner.* In this
work, Archimedes ranges between arithmetic and astronomy, proving himself in both arenas of research and thus

establishing his reputation,[8] which, in second-century AD Rome, is affirmed by Silius Italicus in his *Punica*:[9]

> Non illum mundi numerasse capacis harenas
> vana fides.

> *Punica* 14.350–51

[That he counted all the grains of sand the world contains is not a vain belief.]

Echoing Catullus and, perhaps implicitly, Archimedes about the vast number of grains of sand, Virgil will make a parallel observation about the great number of names of wines:

> Sed neque quam multae species nec nomina quae sint
> est numerus, neque enim numero comprendere refert;
> quem qui scire uelit, Libyci uelit aequoris idem
> dicere quam multae Zephyro turbentur harenae.[10]

> *Georgics* 2.103–6

[But there is no counting how many types there are nor what their names are, nor in fact does it matter even if one could comprehend this by counting. Should one wish to know, then one would likely also wish to proclaim how many grains of sand on the Libyan coast are tossed by the west wind.]

The same comparison will recur in an intriguing fashion in a passage at the opening of *Ode* 1.28, a learned reference typical of Horace's collection:

> Te maris et terrae numeroque carentis harenae
> mensorem cohibent, Archyta.

> *Odes* 1.28.1–2

[They say that you, Archytas, were the one who measured the sea and the numberless sand of the earth.]

Qui . . . terrae mensorem is a way of saying "one who practices geometry," and thus it does not seem improbable that the name of Archimedes, which as we have seen had, for metrical reasons, a good deal of difficulty of finding its way into verse, has been exchanged to that of Archytas, the great Pythagorean philosopher who did not ultimately even address the number of grains of sand. The hypothesis is cautiously advanced by Nisbet and Hubbard in the first volume of their commentary:

> In his *Psammites* or *Sand Reckoner* Archimedes achieved the impossible: he showed that the sand could be counted even if the whole universe were filled with it . . . There is no evidence that Archytas had previously counted the sand; Archimedes does not mention him, and his own treatise is said to show characteristic originality. But it would be rash to assume that Horace has simply confused Archytas and Archimedes. Obviously he had heard of the *Psammites*. So Horace ascribed the counting of the sand to Archytas, as the sort of thing that a mathematician did. A poet would have no respect for facts in a matter of this kind.[11]

In conclusion, one should recall that Archimedes was a personal friend of Conon, with whom the scientist himself recalls a deep and constant friendship, mourning his death at the beginning of his treatise *The Squaring of the Parabola*. In the verses of Catullus, as well as later, in those of the young Virgil, the personality of Archimedes and of Conon could, in the field of science, represent well the two cities of Syracuse and Alexandria, connected in the literary field by two shining lights such as the poets Theocritus and Callimachus.[12]

X

THE "MYTH" OF ARCHIMEDES, YESTERDAY AND TODAY

Even during Archimedes' own lifetime a series of pleasant but (at least partly) fanciful anecdotes were told about him. As we saw in chapter 1, some of these have been transmitted to us by Plutarch. According to that Greek biographer, a Siren who accompanied Archimedes at all times put him under a spell, because of which he frequently forgot to eat or to attend to his other physical needs. According to this obviously embellished account, the scientist's friends had to force him to bathe, while Archimedes simply continued to draw geometric figures on his own dirty body (*Life of Marcellus* 17; cf. plate 2).

In his succinct and admirable study, the nineteenth-century Italian mathematician Antonio Favaro affirmed that Archimedes' preeminence "touched on the boundaries of legend."[1] It is no surprise that the possessor of such talent became virtually a legend throughout history from antiquity to the Renaissance. He remains such in the present day and no doubt will continue to hold such prominence in the future.

An example of his fame, as we saw earlier, can be found
in the account of the Roman general Marcus Claudius
Marcellus, who went so far as to apologize for the kill-
ing of Archimedes, even building him a tomb adorned with
a sphere in a cylinder, reflecting the name of Archimedes'
work entitled *On the Sphere and the Cylinder*. Cicero
makes a particular reference to it when, a century and a
half later, he speaks about how he had made a small survey
and archaeological discovery [plate 15]:

> When I was quaestor [75 BC], I discovered his tomb,
> completely surrounded and covered with brambles and
> branches, of the existence of which the Syracusans had
> been ignorant in as much as they denied entirely that
> it even existed. I recalled certain trifling six-measure
> verses, which I had once learned were inscribed upon
> his tomb, declaring that a sphere with a cylinder was
> placed on top of the tomb. Moreover, as I was looking
> around one day at all the tombs—as outside of the Agri-
> gentine gate there is a large number of tombs—I spied a
> small column that was not protruding very far from the
> bushes, on which there stood the image of a sphere and
> a cylinder.
>
> Immediately I told the Syracusans (the most notable
> citizens were with me) that I thought it was exactly what
> I was looking for. Slaves with sickles were sent out to
> clear away obstructions from the place, offering open
> access to the spot. We approached the front side of the
> pedestal: we saw an inscription with just about half the
> lines visible; for which the verses were corroded at each
> end. So one of the most famous cities of Magna Grae-
> cia, which had at one time even been the most learned,
> would have been ignorant of the existence of the tomb
> of her most brilliant citizen, unless a man from Arpinum
> had made it known to them. [*Tusculan Disputations*
> 5.64–66]

The fame of Archimedes grew throughout antiquity, manifesting itself frequently in Latin poetry, as we saw in the previous chapter. This reputation was advanced, also, throughout the medieval period. In the sixth century, Cassiodorus testifies that Boethius had translated some of his treatises, but no fragments from these can be accurately strung together. Later, in the ninth century, Arabic writers translated some of Archimedes' works, and his reputation waxed so great in Islamic culture that several spurious works were published under his name.[2] In the Greek Middle Ages, particularly in the twelfth century, the first testimonies of widespread references to his *On Burning Mirrors* appear. In this treatise Archimedes demonstrated how sunlight can be focused on one point so as to create fire. This long-distance defensive weapon was employed in the defense of Syracuse when hostile Roman ships were approaching at a great distance (see above, chap. 8).

In the West, during the middle of the thirteenth century, the Dominican Friar William of Moerbeke completed his translation of most of the corpus of Archimedes from Greek into Latin. This translation was housed in the papal library of Viterbo, though various leaflets of Archimedes had already previously appeared in the Western translations from Arabic. Indeed, Gerard of Cremona in Toledo, Spain, had so rendered the *Measurement of a Circle* before (1187). The translation of William of Moerbeke, to which he affixed his autograph (Codex 1850 Ottobonianus Latinus of the Biblioteca Vaticana), was likely the result of widespread admiration for Archimedes in the late medieval period as the Renaissance began to unfold. This is also true of one later prepared by Jacopo of Cremona on behalf of Pope Nicholas V in the middle of the fifteenth century [see fig. 4].

Unfortunately, the Greek codices from which these translators worked have been lost. These included the so-called B codex, in the case of William of Moerbeke, and more importantly the A codex for Jacopo of Cremona, which also belonged to Giorgio Valla but disappeared shortly after 1550. From the A manuscript were derived the Greek copies of Archimedes preserved today in the most important libraries in Europe, such as Codex 305 of the Biblioteca Marciana in Venice, which once belonged to Cardinal Bessarion, dating back to circa 1450 [see fig. 5]. Our knowledge of Archimedes also greatly improved when, in Istanbul in 1906, a palimpsest dating to the Byzantine period was discovered. In it, among other things, was a copy of Archimedes' *Method*, hitherto believed to have been lost (cf. chap. 8, where this is discussed more fully).

The first complete edition of the then-known works of Archimedes was published in Basel in 1544 [see fig. 18], together with the late-antique commentary of Eutocius and the Latin translation of Jacopo of Cremona, corrected by the German mathematician Johannes Müller of Königsberg (whose Italian pseudonym was Regiomontano). From that time on, the writings of Archimedes, formerly available only to a few dozen intellectuals, were read by a much wider audience, including hundreds of scholars. Such dissemination gave scientific studies an enormous boost in the Renaissance:

> The writings of Archimedes that aroused greatest admiration were, not surprisingly, those that deal with the calculation of areas and volumes. Indeed, at first, as other masterpieces of Greek art and science already had, they produced in some readers a feeling of despondency, that is to say the impression of being faced with heights of discovery that no one ever could surpass. Indeed, prior to Archimedes, not even the great mathematicians had produced substantial new mathematical contributions. Nevertheless, this period was to be an important chapter in the history of mathematics that later gave

birth to major developments carried out in the seventeenth century. Yet Archimedes' ancient imprint would bear upon the new research of modern science, as well.[3]

Among the admirers of Archimedes were Piero della Francesca,[4] Luca Pacioli, Leonardo da Vinci, Niccolò Tartaglia, Federico Commandino,[5] and ultimately Galileo Galilei, who claims to have read and studied Archimedes' works "with unceasing astonishment." Indeed Galileo cites the ancient scientist explicitly more than one hundred times, going as far as to describe him as "superhuman," "inimitable," and "a man most divine" (*superhumanus, inimitabilis, divinissimus*). For his technical creativity Galileo regarded himself as similar to Archimedes, as he was depicted in the ancient accounts, for Archimedes—the inventor of the pump screw, ship-destroying machines of war, hydraulic winches, planetariums, and so forth—served as the classic example of one who could employ mathematics for use in everyday life.

The intellectual power of the Syracusan scientist is connected with the originality and fecundity of his research and the way he had used mathematics to treat the problems of physics (e.g., in the formation of the concept of rectilinear motion by force of inertia). Nevertheless, serious study of Archimedes is difficult and demands a constant reinterpretation of his texts. This stipulation made Archimedes, in the Renaissance, one of the main driving forces in the great renewal of science that spilled over into subsequent centuries. The seventeenth century, for example, saw the first criticisms of his method of exhaustion. Though that method could not be accused of a lack of rigor, it was criticized for not making clear how to reach conclusions quickly and efficiently, thus appearing to have a kind of ineffective sterility. Thus, Johannes Kepler, the seventeenth-century German astronomer, while recognizing the general value of Archimedes' research, tried to expound in a more modern way the main points of the treatise *On the Sphere and the Cylinder,* specifically introducing "infinitely small" magnitudes (the first stage of today's infinitesimal analysis) in his *Stereometria Archimedis* ("Art of Measurement of Archimedes," 1615).

The founders of modern science between the seventeenth and eighteenth centuries expanded the role attributed to Archimedes, whose figure assumed a paradigmatic status in the very time in which the precision of his writings began to be called into question. Shortly after Kepler, in fact, Isaac Newton shows great respect for Archimedes, regarding him almost as an equal, though he does not feel the need to compare his own method of demonstration with that of Archimedes.[6]

The most creative phase of the influence of the Syracusan scientist in mathematics and physics begins to expire just when the infinitesimal analysis, of which he was the true forefather, begins to supplant the geometry of indivisibles:

> [The legacy of Archimedes] is like a coin with two faces: on the obverse there is the canonization of Archimedes and of his work, while on the reverse, there is virtually nothing, representing an almost total obliviousness towards the Archimedes who had such an impact on Renaissance humanism; that Archimedes has left the scene entirely.[7]

During the nineteenth and twentieth centuries and even today the influence and vitality of Archimedes tends to be found in erudite studies by classical philologists more than in the mere myths about him [plates 10A and 10B]. For example, in his famous critical edition of 1880–1881 and 1910–1915, Johan Ludvig Heiberg states that Archimedes was the leader and teacher among the most prominent men of his day (*summis ingeniis dux et magister fuit*). In Italy, and especially in Sicily, the scientist was seen as a source of local and national pride, thanks to his famous military defense of Syracuse. Particularly in the nineteenth century, when Europe was infected by a strong and pervasive sense of nationalism, Archimedes came to be regarded as the prime representative of the scientific knowledge not just of Syracuse but of all of Italy.

Today the ancient scientist is considered both a great theoretician and a model of scientific ingenuity [fig. 25].[8] It cannot be overemphasized that, as an inventor, Archimedes was truly inimitable, inasmuch as he obtained results that were both innovative and original. He presented these results simply and without grand eloquence, maintaining a tone of professionalism that transcends mere self-confidence, revealing the enormous potential of human intelligence. These aspects of his character reveal that Archimedes embodied a balance of genius and the quest of discovery, an issue reflected in the Enlightenment debates about genius and the discovery of truth [fig. 26]. Nevertheless, the numerous anecdotes that grew up around his persona, combined with relatively haphazard dissemination of his works, have caused the historical Archimedes to be tainted by or even blended with mythical characters more than to be able to take his appropriate place at the table with the other great minds of history. As Russo has duly noted, Archimedes "is remembered, yes, but as a legendary character, outside of history."[9]

The ancient mathematician has been transformed time and again for the youthful imagination in extraordinary representations of animated cartoons, as in the Russian series in which Archimedes seeks to enamor Russian children with many of his less complex geometric theorems [fig. 27]. Even more delightful is a character introduced in the early sixties in a Disney comic strip and cartoon called, in Italian, *Archimede Pitagorico*. That series presented the cartoon character as the altruistic inventor of far-fetched

FIGURE 25

One of the more serious and established Italian mathematical journals significantly bears the name of the Syracusan scientist.

FIGURE 26

Greek stamp of 1983, on the "European Idea," dedicated to the scientist. Archimedes is depicted completing his studies in geometry. In the background, an explanatory design recalls the physicist's theory of displacement: "a body dipped in a liquid returns from the bottom toward the top with a thrust equal to the displaced weight of the liquid." The face of Archimedes is taken from a bust housed in the Naples Museum once believed to represent the scientist but now known to depict the Spartan king Archidamus III [fig. 3].

FIGURE 27

An image taken from the Russian animated cartoon Kolja, Olja, and Archimedes, *1972, by Jurij Prytkov.*

machines designed to tackle the most difficult problems, even something as improbable as a device used to remove a hammer stuck in someone's head. A helper named "Edi" (short, no doubt for Thomas Edison), whose head is a lightbulb, often accompanies this heroic Archimedes [cf. fig. 28]. Their imaginary inventions develop from modern research, reflecting discoveries, not so much in the field of mathematics or of abstract speculation, but in the tangible elements of everyday life, such as hot buttered popcorn or three-dimensional television. Such achievements would certainly not have displeased the ancient scientist, though his name in the same American cartoon might have, for it is the rather pedestrian Gyro Gearloose, attended not by "Edi" but by a bulb-headed character named "Little Helper." Fortunately, another Archimedes appears in the American Walt Disney production of *The Sword in the Stone*, where he is none other than Merlin's sarcastic assistant, an owl with a somewhat caustic but not inappropriate sense of humor. That is the cartoon version of Archimedes that children of the English-speaking world have made a part of their childhood memories, a character both providing, and keeping for himself, the last laugh.

FIGURE 28

*The Pythagorean Archimedes of the Italian comic strips
(reproduced by the kind permission of Walt Disney Italia).*

NOTES

CHAPTER I

1   Antonio Favaro, *Archimede* (Genoa: Formiggini, 1912), 52–53 (translator's rendering, hic et passim).

2   Reviel Netz, "Archimedes," in *Storia della Scienza*, ed. Sandro Petruccioli et al., vol. 1 (Rome: Istituto della Enciclopedia Italiana, 2001), 781.

3   Attilio Frajese, ed., *Opere di Archimede*, Classici della Scienza (Turin: UTET, 1974), 20.

4   Discussed further in chap. 8.

5   In the planetarium the movements of the sun, the moon and the five then-known planets (Mercury, Venus, Mars, Jupiter, Saturn, i.e., those visible to the naked eye) were imitated exactly. The machine could be used to represent the formation of the eclipse: "And for this reason the invention of Archimedes must be admired because he had figured out how, in the midst of very dissimilar motions, one single rotation could maintain the course of the planets, though they be unequal and various" (Cicero, *De re publica* 1.21). Arab sources mention a work of Archimedes, *On the Construction of the Sphere*, in which the scientist seems to have given specific instructions to make the planetarium.

CHAPTER II

1   The letter π comes from the first letter of the Greek word "periph-
     ery" (i.e., circumference), but its use as a mathematical symbol
     dates back to the seventeenth century; before that, among the
     many different symbols employed, one also finds the Latin letter
     "p" used to express the same concept.

2   1 Kings 7:23.

3   Geoffrey E. R. Lloyd, *Greek Science after Aristotle* (New York:
     W. W. Norton, 1973), 44.

4   Gaetano Fichera, "Rigore e profondità nella concezione di Archi-
     mede della matematica quantitativa," in *Archimede: Mito, Tra-
     dizione, Scienza*. Atti del convegno (Siracusa–Catania, 9–12
     ottobre 1989), ed. Corrado Dollo (Florence: Olschki, 1992), 4.
     There is, moreover, no lack of linguistic arguments (e.g., the disap-
     pearance of every trace of Doric dialect spoken by Archimedes in
     his own time) and issues associated with his works' content (e.g.,
     the second and third theorems are presented in inverse order to
     how they should be) to sustain the notion that the work that has
     come to us is not the original but a redaction edited in late antiq-
     uity. It has even been suggested that this edition could have been
     produced by Hypatia, a mathematician and Neoplatonic philoso-
     pher who died at the hands of Christians in Alexandria in 415
     AD. Such is the hypothesis of Wilbur Richard Knorr in his *Textual
     Studies in Ancient and Medieval Geometry* (Boston: Birkhäuser,
     1989).

5   Fichera, "Rigore e profondità," 9.

6   Moreover, the depth and complexity of the work of Archimedes in
     its historical and scientific reality was able to be understood only
     upon the discovery of his treatise *The Method on Mechanical The-
     orems* at the beginning of the twentieth century (to be discussed
     further in chap. 8).

CHAPTER III

1   An interesting treatment of the argument can be found in an article
     by the physicist Dionigi Galletto, "La teoria della leva nell'opera di
     Archimede e la critica ad essa rivolta da Mach," in Dollo, *Archi-
     mede*, 415–75. Further on Mach's criticisms, cf. Eduard Jan Dijk-
     sterhuis, *Archimedes,* trans. C. Dikshoorn (Princeton: Princeton
     University Press, 1987), 291–96.

2   Archimedes' famous expression "Give me a place to stand and I
     will move the world" (δῶς μοι πᾶ στῶ καὶ τὰν γᾶν κινάσω) is recorded

by Pappus of Alexandria (a mathematician of the 4C AD), by Simplicius of Cilicia (6C) in his commentary on Aristotelean physics, and by the Byzantine John Tzetzes (12C), who mentions it in the Doric dialect spoken by Archimedes in Syracuse (*Various Stories 35*, 129–30: this was also called the *Chiliads* because it was divided into sections of a thousand lines each).

3   For a mathematical description of these, see Dijksterhuis, *Archimedes*, 405–8.

CHAPTER IV

1   See Maria Losito, "La ricostruzione della volute del capitello ionico vitruviano nel Rinascimento italiano," in the appendix of *Vitruvio, De architectura*, ed. Pierre Gros, trans. Antonio Corso and Elisa Romano (Turin: Enandi, 1997), 1409–28.

2   Galileo's enthusiasm for "the marvelous spirals of Archimedes" is evident when in 1638 the Pisan scientist, almost to the letter, reprises the proposition of Archimedes at the beginning of his treatment of uniform motion (*de motu aequabili*) in his *Discourses and Mathematical Demonstrations* relating to *Two New Sciences* (Day I, VIII).

3   Netz, "Archimede," 789.

4   An interesting version of the episode is found later in *Carmen de ponderibus et mensuris* ("Poetry of weights and measures"), passed on to us under the name of the sixth-century Latin grammarian Priscus. In all probability it goes back at least a century before (for this suggestion, see Dimitris K. Raïos, "Archimède, Ménélaos d'Alexandrie et le *Carmen de pondenbus et mensuris*," in *Contributions à l'histoire des sciences* [Ionnina: University of Ioannina, 1989]).

5   The weight of the displaced fluid can be found mathematically; it is represented by the equation $W = mg$, where the mass (m) can be expressed in terms of the density and its volume, $m = pV$. Hence, $W = pVg$.

6   *On Floating Bodies*, book I, at the end of proposition 7. *On Floating Bodies* was known only through the Latin translation that Willem van Moerbeke made in the Middle Ages, but the lacuna happened in much of the palimpsest found in the beginning of the twentieth century at Istanbul and now preserved in Baltimore (discussed in chap. 8).

7   Lloyd, *Greek Science after Aristotle*, 47.

CHAPTER V

1   Netz, "Archimede," 781.

2   A copious note on this premise of Archimedes by Attilio Frajese can be found in its edition of *The Works*, 61–68.

3   Netz, "Archimede," 781.

4   Thus Archimedes says in his letter to Dositheus with which the treatise opens. Cf. Dijksterhuis, *Archimedes*, 109–10.

5   See my "Nota Critica ad Eratostene," 35.4 in A. W. B. Powell, *Rendiconti dell'Instituto Lombardo* 96 (1962): 96–100.

CHAPTER VI

1   "Yet we find Archimedes devising a notation that allows him to name numbers up to the number we should represent by 1 followed by 80,000 million million ciphers—that is $10^8 \cdot 10^{16}$—a number which he describes, with striking economy, in seven Greek words . . . The actual solution he arrives at is that the number in question is not greater than the number we should express as 10^{63}" (Lloyd, *Greek Science after Aristotle*, 42–43).

2   Netz, "Archimede," 790.

3   Dijksterhuis, *Archimedes*, 360.

4   As we saw in the preceding chapter, Archimedes, a slightly younger contemporary of Aristarchus, refers to this theory in the introduction to his work *The Sand Reckoner*: "Aristarchus of Samos published a book of certain hypotheses, in which he shows that the universe is many times greater than the radius equal to the line between the center of the sun and the earth's core. He hypothesizes that the fixed stars and the sun remain unmoved; that the earth is borne round the sun on the circumference of a circle." See Lloyd, *Greek Science after Aristotle*, 53–54.

5   The *Book of Dilemmas* is also frequently attributed to Archimedes' taste for games, though it is conveyed to us only in an Arabic version translated into Latin in the seventeenth century. These are propositions that concern the chords of a circle, but also two particular calculations of area known as the "salt cellar" and the "shoemaker's knife."

6   The fractions of a square as shown in a fragment of the Arab Archimedes were respectively 1/16, 1/48, 1/6, 1/24, 1/24, 1/12, 1/12, 1/24, 1/48, 1/24, (1/2) (1/6) + (1/2) (1/8), 1/12, 1/12, 1/12.

7   Number XVIII of the edition of Roger P. H. Green (Oxford, 1999), 147, ll. 39–50.

8   This is the well-argued hypothesis of Reviel Netz, Fabio Acerbi,

and Nigel Wilson in "Towards a Reconstruction of Archimedes' 'Stomachion,'" *Sciamus* 5 (2004): 6–99.

CHAPTER VII

1 Lionel Casson, *Ships and Seamanship in the Ancient World*, 2nd ed. (Princeton: Princeton University Press, 1986), 185.
2 *Deipnosophistae* 5.206d–209b.
3 Vitruvio, *De architectura*, vol. 2, 1383n118.
4 Thus Bertrand Gille in his chapter entitled "Machines," in *A History of Technology*, ed. Charles Singer et al., vol. 2 (Oxford, New York: Oxford University Press, 1957), 633.
5 The account of Livy is also interesting: "While Archimedes was an unparalleled observer of the sky and the stars, even more extraordinary is that he was an inventor and manufacturer of weapons and war machines, with which he would with no great effort make easy sport whatever offensive the enemy, with enormous expenditure might orchestrate; . . . he equipped, with every type of mechanism, the walls that ran along the uneven hills. . . That wall against which the sea broke was besieged by Marcellus with sixty quinqueremes . . . but against this armada Archimedes stationed on the walls devices of various sizes. He was flinging masses of enormous weight at the ships that were farther away, while he struck those closer with weapons capable of launching lighter, and therefore more frequent, projectiles" [*Ab urbe condita* 24.34].
6 Livy continues, in the same chapter: "Some ships were approaching the walls more closely, so that they might not be too close for blows of their weapons: an iron claw was used against these ships; the claw was attached to a strong chain, thrown over the wall on a projecting boom. When, owing to a heavy lead weight, it had fallen back to the ground, it was able to position the ship, stern-down and bow-upwards. Archimedes then let it fall down suddenly, sending the ship hurled from the walls, to the great consternation of the sailors. It thus plunged in the waves with such force that, even if it fell straight down, it took on a great deal of water."
   Polybius, in the sixth chapter of his fragmentary eighth book, also describes the "claw" designed by Archimedes: "These machines then . . . flung stones large enough to scatter from the prow those attacking and at the same time lowered a claw of iron tied to a chain. With this he who maneuvered the arm, by which he could lay hold of the prow, would drive down the heel of the device inside the wall, so lifting the ship's prow straight up, and putting the boat upon its stern. Thus he made the heel of the machine

stationary and then scattered the 'catch' from the machine using a release trigger. Once this happened, some boats fell on one side, while others were turned over. Most, however, with their prows dropped from a height, plunged into the sea and, filled with water, were thus thrown into disarray."

7   Apuleius "On Magic," chap. 16: "And there are many other phenomena that the Syracusan Archimedes treats in a large volume: though he was, in every geometric science, wonderful beyond all others for precision, this man is perhaps most memorable for having looked into a looking glass often and carefully" (*quod inspexerat speculum saepe ac diligenter,* where Apuleius clearly offers a paronomasia on looked, *inspexerat,* and looking glass, *speculum*).

8   Ioannes Zonaras (*Epitome Historiarum* 9.4) and John Tzetzes (*Chiliades* 103–28) both mention Archimedes' mirrors. Before them, Anthemius of Tralles, the sixth-century architect of the church of Hagia Sophia in Constantinople and a good mathematician himself, wrote a treatise *On Burning Mirrors,* in which he refers to Archimedes. The Greek version of this treatise is lost, but an Arabic version survives; this version has been translated into French (Roshdi Rashed, ed., *Les Catoptriciens Grecs,* vol. 1, *Les miroirs ardents* [Paris: Les Belles Lettres, 2000], 303, 309, 317, esp. 319).

9   Georgius Helmreich, *Galeni de temperamentis libri III* (Leipzig: Teubner, 1904), 93.16 = Karl Gottlob Kühn, *Claudii Galeni Opera Omnia* (Leipzig: Prostat in Officina Libraria Car. Cnoblochii, 1821–1833), 1.657.16.

10   David L. Simms discusses this in "Archimedes and the Burning Mirrors of Syracuse" and "Galen on Archimedes: Burning Mirrors or Burning Pitch?" in *Technology and Culture* 18 (1977): 1–24, 32; (1991): 91–96.

CHAPTER VIII

1   The ink of the original palimpsest had been cleared off using lemon juice and a pumice stone; fortunately, this cleansing method did not remove the original text completely, and much has remained readable with a magnifying glass. In recent years researchers at Stanford University have employed X-ray technology to reproduce the original text, specifically using a synchrotron accelerator to try to bring to light more of the text. Much of the success of this project is owed to the enthusiastic research physicist Uwe Bergmann of the Stanford Kavli Institute for Particle Astrophysics and

Cosmology (Stanford Linear Accelerator Center). Bergmann discovered that the original text was written with an ink that contains iron, and in the laboratory the synchrotron helped to detect a small quantity of iron in proteins on the page, allowing Bergmann to reconstruct better the words of the palimpsest. Some sheets newly deposited in Baltimore are then passed to Silicon Valley, where the reading of ancient texts also proceeds slowly with the synchrotron, painstakingly deciphering each letter of each word of the text. Accordingly, after so many centuries of the text's invisibility, it seems that one must yet remain patient until new information can be revealed by this method. Further, see http://academicearth.org/lectures/archimedes-ancient-text-uwe-bergmann.

2   For this proposition, in particular, the lines have only recently been interpreted in a satisfactory manner by Reviel Netz, Ken Saito, and Natalie Tchernetska, "A New Reading of *Method* Proposition 14: Preliminary Evidence from the Archimedes Palimpsest," pt. 1, *Sciamus* 2 (2001): 9–29; pt. 2, *Sciamus* 3 (2002): 109–25.

3   Lucio Russo, *The Forgotten Revolution: Greek Scientific Thought and Modern Science*, trans. Silvio Levy (Berlin: Springer, 2004), 72.

4   Frajese, *Opere di Archimede*, 561.

5   So Giuseppe Cambiano concludes his article "Scoperta e dimostrazione in Archimede," in Dollo, *Archimede*, 21–41 (translator's rendering).

CHAPTER IX

1   Otto Skutsch, *The Annals of Q. Ennius* (Oxford, 1985), XXII.

2   *Ille, novus pluuias Titan ut proderet ortu / fuscatis tristis radiis. Ille, haereat anne / pendeat instabilis tellus, cur foedere certo / hunc affusa globum Tethys circumliget undis, / nouerat atque una pelagi lunaeque labores, / et pater Oceanus qua lege effunderet aestus* [He knew how the sun in its rising portended rain, though it was gloomy with dull rays; he knew whether the earth clings where it hangs in space or is unstable in its position; he even knew why, with unalterable law, the sea, poured forth over the earth, surrounds it with its waters; he understood, too, the labors of the moon and tide, and by what law Father Ocean governs the seas' surges, *Punica* 14.344–49].

3   Further references appear in Cicero in particular in *De finibus* 5.19.50 and the *Oratio Secunda in Verrem* 4.58.131 (on the death of Archimedes).

4   Graham Zanker, who believes that dialogue between scientists and physicians must have been facilitated by the Museum at Alexandria, specifically calls attention to the epigrams of Eratosthenes on the duplication of the cube (fr. 35 Powell) as "a delightful essay on the versification of mathematics" in the fourth chapter entitled "The Appeal to Science," in his *Realism in Alexandrian Poetry: A Literature and Its Audience* (London: Croom Helm, 1987), 113–31, 124, 126.

5   See R. Alden Smith, *Virgil* (London: Blackwell, 2010), 44–45.

6   Even in his early works, Virgil has no shortage of numerical games. For example, *Eclogue* 3.71: *aurea mala decem misi; cras altera mittam* ("I sent ten golden apples; tomorrow it will send another ten," where *altera* ["another"] is the same adjective referring to ten used by Catullus in 5.8). A further example can be seen in *Eclogue* 8.73–75, 77: *terna tibi haec primum triplici diversa colore / licia circumdo, terque haec circum altaria / effigiem duco; numerus deus impare gaudet. / . . . / Necte tribus nodis ternos, Amarylli, colores* ("I first connect these three lines, distinct by their threefold colors, and thrice I bring an effigy around these altars. A god rejoices in the uneven number . . . Connect the three colors, Amaryllis, with three knots"). Further, see Smith, *Virgil*, 82.

7   Harry L. Levy once pointed this out in his article "Catullus, 5, 7–11 and the Abacus," *American Journal of Philosophy* 52 (1941): 222–24: "According to my interpretation, Catullus thinks of himself as keeping score of Lesbia's kisses on an abacus. First a pebble in the thousands column, then one in the hundreds, then another in the thousands, and another in the hundreds, then still another in the thousands, and one in the hundreds, and then, when the thrice-told tale is done, the lovers shake the board violently (*conturbabimus*), the pebbles fly in all directions, and the score is forever obliterated."

8   His fame does not suggest that the Romans had a detailed grasp of the proofs of Archimedes, who concluded his work with a somewhat skeptical but warm (and frank) address to his reader: "These things then, King Gelon, I think will seem incredible to many who are inexperienced in mathematics, but will be credible, through demonstrations, to those who are versed in mathematics and who have meditated on the distances and sizes of the earth, the sun, the moon and the whole universe. Therefore, I felt it was good for you to know these things."

9   In fact Calpurnius Siculus, a few years later, called attention to the difficulty of such a calculation: *Qui numerare velit quam multa sub arbore nostro / poma legam, tenues citius numerabit harenas* ("He who wants to count how many fruits I gather beneath my tree, could far more quickly count grains of fine sand," 2.73–74). At the end of the first century AD, Hyginus Gromaticus, too, admired Archimedes' large numbers: *Nam et Archimedem, uirum praeclari ingenio et magnarum rerum inuentorem, ferunt scripsisse, quantum arenarum capere posset mundus, si repleretur* ("For also they say that Archimedes, a man with outstanding talent and an inventor of great things, had written how much sand the world could hold, if it should be filled up with it"). From *Corpus Agrimensorum Romanorum*, ed. Carl Olof Thulin (Leipzig: Teubner, 1913), 148.

10 Virgil adds to the difficulty of counting the number of the grains of sand in Africa the entirely immeasurable number of the waves rolling in upon the shores of the Ionian Sea (*quot Ionii veniant ad litora fluctus*, 108), a comparison that in turn echoes passages of Apollonius Rhodius (*Argonautica* 4.214–15) and Theocritus (*Idyll* 16.60–61).

11 *A Commentary on Horace: Odes, Book 1* (Oxford: Clarendon, 1970), 321.

12 According to Josef Svennung, *Catulls Bildersprache* (Uppsala: Lundequist, 1945), 84–85, some verses of Catullus' seventh poem are modeled on a passage from Theocritus' *Idyll* 30: "He who would believe that he can vanquish Eros, that craftsman of deceit, would also believe that he could easily ascertain how many times nine the stars above us are," 25–27). This would be a further example of the meaningful, if less than frequent, Catullan resonances of Theocritus in the Roman poet's corpus.

CHAPTER X

1   Favaro, *Archimede*, 12.

2   In medieval texts Archimedes' name was sometimes collapsed to Arsamithes or Archimenedes. However, in all probability, there are several original treatises that have not come down to us in Greek but were published in recent years in Arabic versions. These are *The Construction of a Regular Heptagon*, *On the Construction of Water Clocks*, and *On Mutually Tangent Circles* (the last of these has been edited by Yvonne Dold-Samplonius, in vol. 4 of *Archimedis Opera Omnia* [Stuttgart: Teubner, 1975]).

3   Ludovico Geymonat, "Archimede e il metodo infinitesimale," *Illustrazione Scientifica* 13 (1950): 17.

4   Cf. James R. Banker, "A Manuscript of the Works of Archimedes in the Hand of Piero della Francesca," *The Burlington Magazine* 147 (2005): 165–69. In the autograph of his *Treatise on the Abacus*, now in the Biblioteca Medicea Laurenziana in Florence, Piero recopied over seventy pages of the Latin translation of Archimedes preserved in Florence's Biblioteca Riccardiana, which confirms his knowledge of that language and his extraordinary interest in Greek mathematics. Further, see Judith Veronica Field, *The Invention of Infinity: Mathematics and Art in the Renaissance* (New York: Oxford University Press, 1997), 62–65.

5   Tartaglia and Commandino edited two partial but important collections of Archimedes, published in Venice in the years 1543 and 1558, respectively.

6   See Massimo Galluzzi, "La lettura di Archimede nell'opera di Newton," in Dollo, *Archimede,* 312.

7   Paolo Casini, "Archimede e gli storici del Settecento," in Dollo, *Archimede*, 321.

8   See on these issues in particular the essay by Gianni Micheli, "Il mito di Archimede nell'Ottocento e nel Novecento in Italia," in Dollo, *Archimede*, 335–45.

9   Russo, *The Forgotten Revolution*, 6.

BIBLIOGRAPHY

Archimedis opera omnia cum commentariis Eutocii. Edited by Johan Ludvig Heiberg. 3 vols. Leipzig: Teubner, 1880–1881, 2nd ed. 1910–1915 [*corrigenda adiecit* Evangelos S. Stamatis, Stuttgart: Teubner, 1972, expanded with a fourth volume, containing *On Mutually Tangent Circles*, a treatise extant only in medieval Arabic translation, by Yvonne Dold-Samplonius et al., Stuttgart: Teubner, 1975].

Clagett, Marshall. *Archimedes in the Middle Ages.* Vol. 1, Madison: University of Wisconsin Press, 1964; Vols. 2–5, Philadelphia: American Philosophical Society, 1976–1984.

Dijksterhuis, Eduard Jan. *Archimedes.* Translated by C. Dikshoorn. Princeton: Princeton University Press, 1987.

Dollo, Corrado, ed. *Archimede: Mito, Tradizione, Scienza.* Atti del convegno (Siracusa–Catania, 9–12 ottobre 1989). Florence: Olschki, 1992.

Favaro, Antonio. *Archimede.* Genoa: Formiggini, 1912.

Frajese, Attilio, ed. *Opere di Archimede.* Classici della Scienza. Turin: UTET, 1974.

Galluzzi, Paolo. *Archimede e la storia delle matematiche nella Galleria degli Uffizi*. Milan: Arnaldo Lombardi, 1989.

Geymonat, Ludovico. "Archimede e il metodo infinitesimal." *Illustrazione Scientifica* 13 (1950): 16–19.

Geymonat, Mario. "Poesia e scienza in Virgilio: dalla III egloga al VI libro dell'Eneide." In *Letteratura e riflessione filosofica nel mondo greco-romano: Atti del corso d'aggiornamento per docenti di latino e greco del Canton Ticino*, edited by Giancarlo Reggi, 165–78. Lugano: Sapiens Editrice, 2005.

Geymonat, Mario, and Franco Minonzio. "Scienza e tecnica nell'Italia romana. I saperi della tradizione e Razionalità matematica, indagine sulla natura e saperi tecnici nella cultura romana." In *Storia della Società Italiana*, vol. 4, 189–458. Milan: Nicola Teti Editore, 1998.

Heath, Thomas L. *The Works of Archimedes, edited in Modern Notation with Introductory Chapters* [1897] *and with a Supplement: Method of Archimedes* [1912]. New York: Dover Publications, 1953.

Jaeger, Mary. *Archimedes and the Roman Imagination*. Ann Arbor: University of Michigan Press, 2008.

Knorr, Wilbur Richard. *Textual Studies in Ancient and Medieval Geometry*. Boston: Birkhäuser, 1989.

Lloyd, Geoffrey E. R. *Greek Science after Aristotle*. New York: W. W. Norton, 1973.

Lo Sardo, Eugenio, ed. *Éureka! Il genio degli antichi*. Exhibition catalog of the Naples National Archaeological Museum. Naples: Electa, 2005.

Minonzio, Franco. "Lo 'Stomachion' di Archimede." *Lettera matematica pristem* 35 (2000): 41–47; 36 (2000): 36–42; 37 (2000): 38–45.

Napolirani, Pier Daniele. "Archimede." In *I grandi della scienza*, vol. 16 of *La scienza*, edited by Enrico Bellone and Enrico Cravetto. Turin: De Agostini-Utet, 2005.

Netz, Reviel. "Archimede." In *Storia della Scienza*, edited by Sandro Petruccioli et al. Vol. 1, chap. 18, 779–90. Rome: Istituto della Enciclopedia Italiana, 2001.

―――. *The Works of Archimedes*, I *(On the Sphere and the Cylinder)*, Translation and Commentary. Cambridge: Cambridge University Press, 2004.

Netz, Reviel, Fabio Acerbi, and Nigel Wilson. "Towards a Reconstruction of Archimedes' 'Stomachion.'" *Sciamus* 5 (2004): 67–99.

Netz, Reviel, and William Noel. *The Archimedes Codex*. London: Weidenfeld & Nicholson, 2007.

Paipetis, Stephanos A., and Marco Ceccarelli. *The Genius of Archimedes—23 Centuries of Influence on Mathematics, Science and Engineering*. Proceedings of an International Conference held at Syracuse, Italy, June 8–10, 2010. History of Mechanism and Machine Science 11. New York: Springer, 2010.

Rufini, Enrico. *Il "Metodo" di Archimede e le origini del calcolo infinitesimale nell'antichità*. Bologna: Zanichelli, 1926; repr. Milan: Feltrinelli, 1961.

INDEX

PLATE I

*The scholar of geometry in meditation, a miniature dating
from the beginning of the 6C AD in the* Codex Arcerianus
of the Agrimensori *(Guelf. 36.23 Aug. 2°, f. 67v, from the Herzog
August Bibliothek in Wolfenbüttel, Germany).*

PLATE 2

Archimedes traces some geometric lines with his finger on his chest, which is anointed with oil. It is one of the paintings executed by Giulio Parigi between 1599 and 1600 for the "Room of the Mathematicians" in the Uffizi Gallery of Florence. The heroic presentation of Archimedes testifies to the rebirth of interest in the Syracusan scientist, as seen also in Tuscany near the end of the 16th century, where we have the arrival of the important Greek codex of his work now preserved in the Biblioteca Medicea Laurenziana. When sixty years or so in the future the Uffizi will dedicate fresh attention to mathematics, Galileo will be celebrated in the corridor facing the gallery like a "New Archimedes." (This and the other reproductions from the Uffizi are used by permission of the Italian Ministry of Cultural Heritage and Activities.)

PLATE 3

"Give me a lever long enough and I will move the world."
The principle of the lever of Archimedes illustrated in an 18th-century
detail of the ceiling of the "Room of the Mathematicians"
in the Uffizi Gallery in Florence.

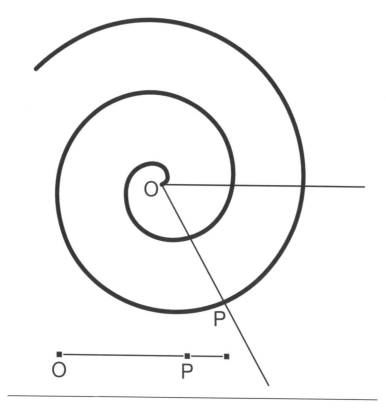

PLATE 4

The spiral (counterclockwise here) is one of the shapes that Archimedes studied with great originality: the semi-straight OP rotates around O and the point P moves with uniform motion around it.

PLATE 5

Archimedes, naked, enthusiastically bounds forth from his bath and heads toward the city crying, "Eureka! Eureka!" ("I've found it! I've found it!"). The scientist is overjoyed to have discovered how to expose the jeweler who had cheated Hiero.This is one of the paintings executed by Giulio Parigi between 1599 and 1600 for the "Room of the Mathematicians" in the Uffizi Gallery in Florence.

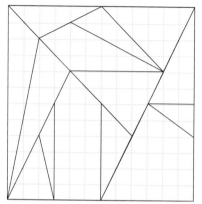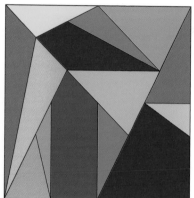

figure A

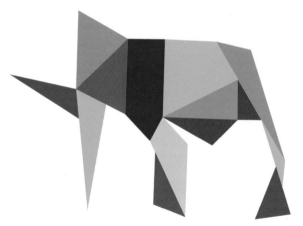

figure B

PLATE 6

*The divisions of a square into sections used for Archimedes' puzzle
game* Stomachion, *formed from 14 pieces (figure A). In figure B the
pieces, which can be arranged in infinite ways, are assembled to form
the shape of an elephant.*

PLATE 7

Model of the ship Syracusia *(as looking toward the prow) constructed in 1980 in Sicily by Guido Vallone. The original was probably 280 cubits long (approximately 120 m), with 40 portals for each group of oars. The ship bore 8 large towers and was encompassed by a balustrade containing numerous weapons of war. The treatise of Archimedes* On Floating Bodies *contained the theoretical basis for the static equilibrium of the bodies immersed in water, and therefore also of giant ships such as the* Syracusia.

PLATE 8

*A ship dragged to land by a screw winch. It is one of the paintings
executed by Giulio Parigi between 1599 and 1600 for the
"Room of the Mathematicians" in the Uffizi Gallery in Florence.*

PLATE 9

Eighteenth-century reconstruction of the "Screw of Archimedes"
(Museum of the History of Science, Florence, inv. 999).
The instrument consisted of a cylinder on the inside of which a large
wooden spiral was positioned. It would have been placed into the water
at an angle and was opened at each end, whereby the water, passing
through the volutes of the spiral, could go up and flow out from the top
of the cylinder. Driven by a crank, the spiral pumped water toward the
height: the inclination of the spiral was adjustable through a winch, but
it could not reach the vertical position because in such a case the water
would have fallen back toward the bottom.

PLATE 10A

The opening-day-release postcard with the stamp issued by the Italian
Postal Service in 2000, which was the "World Mathematical Year."
To mark the continuity between the past and the future of science, an
inscribed sphere is drawn into a cylinder (right), which recalls the classical
measurement of their volume and surface by Archimedes. On the left,
around a part of the terrestrial globe, a Möbius strip is portrayed, which
is one of the most fascinating figures of contemporary geometry.

PLATE 10B

The Fields Medal is the most important international prize for
mathematics (a type of Nobel prize): it comes with a conspicuous sum, in
Canadian dollars, and is awarded every four years on the occasion of the
conference of the International Mathematical Union. On the obverse it
bears a stylized portrait of Archimedes, with his name written in Greek,
encircled by the Latin maxim transire suum pectus mundoque potiri *("To*
transcend the constraints of one's own heart and so grasp the world"),
inspired by verse 392 of the fourth book of the 1st-century astronomical
poet Manilius. The winner of the award and the date are incised in small
letters on the edge of the medallion.

PLATE 11

Trebuchet, one type of catapult or onager used by Archimedes for the defense of Syracuse. It is here depicted in a painting executed by Giulio Parigi between 1599 and 1600 for the "Room of the Mathematicians" in the Uffizi Gallery in Florence.

PLATE 12

The "Iron Claw" of Archimedes in the act of seizing a ship by the prow. This is a painting by Giulio Parigi executed between 1599 and 1600 for the "Room of the Mathematicians" in the Uffizi Gallery in Florence.

PLATE 13

One possible explanation of how Archimedes' "burning mirrors" may have functioned can be seen in this painting by Giulio Parigi, rendered between 1599 and 1600 for the "Room of the Mathematicians" in the Uffizi Gallery in Florence.

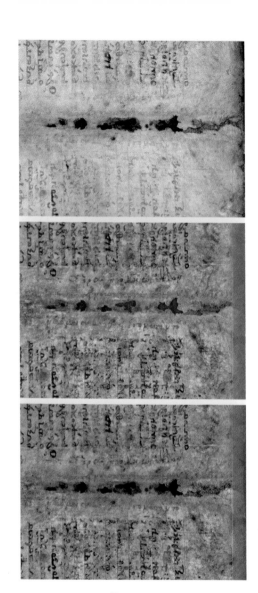

PLATE 14

An eight-line fragment of the Byzantine palimpsest of Archimedes, now housed in the Walters Art Museum in Baltimore. Above, the palimpsest as it appears under natural light; in the middle, in ultraviolet light; below, as reproduced with computer imaging. Under the ultraviolet rays the text absorbs that light and the reading becomes easier (or at least slightly better than nearly impossible). The specialists of the Rochester Institute of Technology in New York, however, have used computers to reproduce also what they call a "pseudo-color" image, in which the ancient writing magically appears in red. (Image taken by Rochester Institute of Technology and Johns Hopkins University. The copyright belongs to the owner of the Archimedes Palimpsest.)

PLATE 15

Cicero Discovering the Tomb of Archimedes at Syracuse,
*painted in 1787 by Pierre-Henri de Valenciennes; now in the Musée des
Augustins of Toulouse in France. In the underbrush Cicero and the elders
delightedly look upon the newfound tomb.*

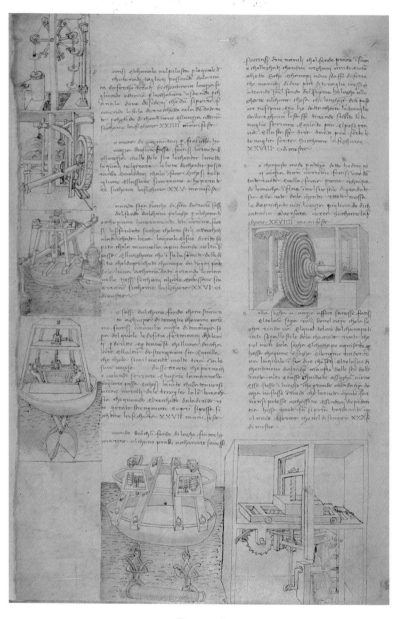

PLATE 16

Miniature of a hydraulic and mechanical design executed by the Sienese painter Francesco di Giorgio Martini at the end of the 14th century in the margins of f. 43v of the manuscript Ashburnham 361 of Biblioteca Medicea Laurenziana of Florence. These drawings represent a disc pump, a hydraulic siphon, a balance elevator, a dredge, a boat for recovery of sunken ships, a hydraulic saw, and a water transport developed from the screw of Archimedes.